DEAR EXECUTOR: A WORKBOOK

MARY JEANNE ANDERSON JONES

ISBN: 978-1-09836-287-4 (paperback)
ISBN: 978-1-09836-288-1 (ebook)

It is my wish to dedicate this workbook

to the memory of my beloved parents

Dorothy Mary Crawford Anderson

and

Buist Murfee Anderson

PRELUDE TO DEAR EXECUTOR: A WORKBOOK

While you were out browsing through a bookstore or happily playing with your computer, you might have asked yourself, "Why should I purchase this *DEAR EXECUTOR: A WORKBOOK*?" and "Why should I then spend hours answering the hundreds of questions pertinent to my life, connections, and assets and liabilities?"

Then think about suddenly dropping dead without having purchased *DEAR EXECUTOR: A WORKBOOK* and not having filled in the vital facts about yourself and your family.

Chaos would reign.

This situation would be particularly painful if you have been the devoted husband or wife, caring for your financial assets and those of your wife or husband without communicating with her or him about the details. Where would your spouse be without the vaguest idea about your family's financial situation or the identity of your lawyer or accountant, the whereabouts of your safe deposit box and its key or combination, or the value of your antiques, and you weren't around to answer the questions? She/he would be in panic mode and of little help to your executor, as are you.

To lessen the crisis incurred by your death by not compounding it with the resulting ignorance about your estate is the reason that you should purchase *DEAR EXECUTOR: A WORKBOOK* and conscientiously spend the multitude of hours required in filling in the pages to the best of your ability. You are protecting your loved ones by providing the knowledge of what's where and who's who for your executor, who in turn is to serve your family after your death.

My earlier but more primitive version of this workbook was a help to me in that it served as a discipline in putting together the whereabouts of my personal information in an orderly fashion. Also, in the event of my becoming incapacitated or dying, I figured that it would be my executor who would reap the benefits and who would bless me for making his/her job far easier and more accurate than it might have been without my input. Hopefully *DEAR EXECUTOR: A WORKBOOK* will be a benefit to you and your executor, while saving your estate many hours of legal fees.

In pursuing this project. I was thankful to have had some brilliant help from several of my favorite people: my son, Rick Jones, my son-in-law, Steve Siegfried, special friends, Buck Rogers and David Morrissey, my other son-in-law, Marc Shafer, who told me about BookBaby's being the publisher of choice, my daughter, Laura Shafer, for editing advice and

Roger Di Tarando, the sculptor who created the marvelous eagle whose portrait is on this cover. I should like to thank the Connecticut Historical Society for allowing me to use their photo of me on this Back Cover and last, but not least I should mention with gratitude the young techs at the Hartford Public Library and West Hartford Library. Without them there would be no *DEAR EXECUTOR: A WORKBOOK* as I could not cope with the pagination. To all I give my special thanks.

DEAR EXECUTOR: A WORKBOOK cannot exactly suit everyone's needs. Most estates must go through probate; most, however, are not required to pay estate taxes to the federal government. Even if you do not think that the amount of your assets will cause your estate to file IRS Form 706 and pay estate taxes, many states have estate or inheritance taxes that may catch you. Your hours spent with this workbook may well aid your executor and lawyer(s) and will hardly have been spent for naught.

Whether or not you think you are going to have to pay estate taxes, look this workbook over carefully. Everyone is different. Skip the pages that are not pertinent. Add pages where you need more space. Feel free to adapt the forms to suit your needs. Try to keep the information reasonably up to date.

Privacy will also be an issue. In considering this *DEAR EXECUTOR: A WORKBOOK* for your estate planning, you may be wondering how to maintain your privacy. Many of the facts that you insert into these forms will contain your most personal information. But they will not be available on the Internet for hackers to hack. They will exist only in the privacy of this workbook.

Therefore, remember that you are under NO obligation to divulge what you have entered on these pages to anyone under ordinary circumstances.

And with this said, I wish you well............

Mary Jeanne Anderson Jones

Now it is your turn.........

INFORMATION PERTINENT TO MY ESTATE

PREPARED BY: _____

DATE: _____

Dear Executor:

I have compiled this edition of *DEAR EXECUTOR: A* WORKBOOK for your benefit and that of my family. May it be of great help to you.

PART I

TABLE OF CONTENTS

PART II

MY OBITUARY

AUTHOR: _____

LOCATION: _____

NEWSPAPER: _____

NEWSPAPER: _____

DATE OF BIRTH: _____

PLACE OF BIRTH: _____

PARENTS, FATHER: _____

MOTHER: _____

SPOUSE/EX-SPOUSE/

SIGNIFICANT OTHER: _____

ADDRESS: _____

EDUCATION: _____

CHILDREN: 1. _____

_____

2. _____

_____

3. _____

_____

RELATIVES: _____

_____

_____

_____

OCCUPATION: _____

MILITARY SERVICE: _____

CHURCH AFFILIATION: _____

LIFE-LONG SPECIAL
INTERESTS: _____

AMERICAN CITIZEN? _____

CONTRIBUTIONS
IN LIEU OF FLOWERS? _____

MY MEMORIAL SERVICE

PUBLIC/PRIVATE:_____

LOCATION: _____

MINISTER: _____

PARTICIPANTS: _____

_____

_____

MUSIC: _____

_____

READINGS:

_____

_____

_____

PROGRAM:

_____

COMMENTS:

_____

_____

_____

_____

MY BURIAL/CREMATION

FUNERAL HOME: _____

CEMETERY: _____

_____

CEMETERY

CONTACT: _____

_____

HEADSTONE: _____

ASHES/URN: _____

MAUSOLEUM: _____

ME

SOCIAL SECURUTY NUMBER: _____

EMAIL ADDRESS: _____

DATE OF BIRTH: _____

PLACE OF BIRTH: _____

_____

BIRTH CERTIFICATE,

LOCATION: _____

MARRIAGE

CERTIFICATE and COPIES of LICENSE,

 LOCATION: _____

SPOUSE: _____

DIVORCE

MEMORANDUM

OF DECISION,

LOCATION: _____

DIVORCE JUDGMENT,

LOCATION: _____

SOCIAL SECURITY CARD,

LOCATION: _____

MEDICARE CARD,

LOCATION: _____

PASSPORT,

LOCATION: _____

COMMENTS:

MY ATTORNEYS

WILL, TRUST, ESTATE

ATTORNEY:

_____

_____

DIVORCE

ATTORNEY:

_____

_____

OTHER:

1. _____

_____

2. _____

_____

LAST WILL and TESTAMENT

LOCATION: _____

_____

DATED: _____

EXECUTOR: _____

BACKUP

EXECUTOR: _____

_____

STATUTORY SHORT FORM
POWER OF ATTORNEY

LOCATION: _____

ATTORNEY-IN-FACT: _____

_____

BACKUP: 1._____

_____

2._____

_____

DURABLE HEALTH CARE POWER OF ATTORNEY

LOCATION: _____

_____

ATTORNEY(S):   1._____

_____

2._____

_____

HEALTH CARE DESIGNEE

NAME: _____

TEL.: _____

ADDRESS: _____

BACKUP: 1. _____

_____

2. _____

_____

REVOCABLE INTER VIVOS TRUST

TRUST AGREEMENT:

        COPY: 1. _____

                     2._____

        TRUSTEE: _____

        BACKUP TRUSTEE(S): 1._____

                    _____

2._____

_____

BENEFICIARIES:

1. _____

2._____

3._____

4._____

5._____

6._____

TERMS:

POST-MORTEM GIFTS TO FAMILY

GIFTS TO FAMLY:

SPOUSE: _____

    1. GIFT: _____

    DATE OF GIFT: _____

    2. GIFT: _____

    DATE OF GIFT: _____

    3. GIFT: _____

    DATE OF GIFT: _____

CHILDREN:

1._____

       GIFT: _____

       DATE OF GIFT: _____

2. _____

       GIFT: _____

       DATE OF GIFT: _____

3._____

        GIFT: _____

        DATE OF GIFT: _____

4._____

        GIFT: _____

        DATE OF GIFT: _____

5._____

        GIFT: _____

        DATE OF GIFT: _____

IRS FORM 709

UNITED STATES GIFT

(and GENERATION-SKIPPING TRANSFER) TAX RETURN

TAXABLE GIFTS:

    1.DONEE: _____

    GIFT: _____

    DATE OF GIFT: _____

    2. **DONEE*:***   _____

    GIFT: _____

    DATE OF GIFT: _____

3. DONEE: _____

GIFT: _____

DATE OF GIFT: _____

4.DONEE: _____

GIFT: _____

DATE OF GIFT: _____

DIRECT SKIP, DONEE:

1. _____

GIFT: _____

DATE OF GIFT: _____

2._____

GIFT:_____

DATE OF GIFT: _____

3._____

GIFT: _____

DATE OF GIFT: _____

4._____

GIFT: _____

DATE OF GIFT: _____

5._____

GIFT: _____

DATE OF GIFT: _____

6._____

GIFT: _____

DATE OF GIFT: _____

INDIRECT SKIPS:

1._____

GIFT: _____

DATE OF GIFT: _____

2._____

GIFT: _____

DATE OF GIFT: _____

3._____

GIFT: _____

DATE OF GIFT: _____

4._____

GIFT: _____

DATE OF GIFT: _____

5._____

GIFT: _____

DATE OF GIFT: _____

TOTAL OF YEAR'S GIFTS: _____

DECEASED SPOUSAL UNUSED EXCLUSION (DSUE):

RECEIVED FROM LAST DECEASED SPOUSE: _____

RECEIVED FROM PREDECEASED SPOUSE(S): _____

SEE COPY OF IRS 2021 FORM 709 ON PAGES FOLLOWING

Form **709**

Department of the Treasury
Internal Revenue Service

United States Gift (and Generation-Skipping Transfer) Tax Return

▶ Go to *www.irs.gov/Form709* for instructions and the latest information.

(For gifts made during calendar year 2021)

▶ See instructions.

OMB No. 1545-0020

2021

Part 1—General Information

1 Donor's first name and middle initial	2 Donor's last name	3 Donor's social security number

4 Address (number, street, and apartment number)	5 Legal residence (domicile)

6 City or town, state or province, country, and ZIP or foreign postal code	7 Citizenship (see instructions)

		Yes	No
8	If the donor died during the year, check here ▶ ☐ and enter date of death _____ , _____ .		
9	If you extended the time to file this Form 709, check here ▶ ☐		
10	Enter the total number of donees listed on Schedule A. Count each person only once ▶		
11a	Have you (the donor) previously filed a Form 709 (or 709-A) for any other year? If "No," skip line 11b		
b	Has your address changed since you last filed Form 709 (or 709-A)?		
12	**Gifts by husband or wife to third parties.** Do you consent to have the gifts (including generation-skipping transfers) made by you and by your spouse to third parties during the calendar year considered as made one-half by each of you? (See instructions.) (If the answer is "Yes," the following information must be furnished and your spouse must sign the consent shown below. **If the answer is "No," skip lines 13–18.**)		
13	Name of consenting spouse		
14	SSN		
15	Were you married to one another during the entire calendar year? See instructions		
16	If line 15 is "No," check whether ☐ married ☐ divorced or ☐ widowed/deceased, and give date. See instructions ▶		
17	Will a gift tax return for this year be filed by your spouse? If "Yes," mail both returns in the same envelope		
18	**Consent of Spouse.** I consent to have the gifts (and generation-skipping transfers) made by me and by my spouse to third parties during the calendar year considered as made one-half by each of us. We are both aware of the joint and several liability for tax created by the execution of this consent.		

Consenting spouse's signature ▶   Date ▶

19	Have you applied a DSUE amount received from a predeceased spouse to a gift or gifts reported on this or a previous Form 709? If "Yes," complete Schedule C		

Part 2—Tax Computation

1	Enter the amount from Schedule A, Part 4, line 11	1	
2	Enter the amount from Schedule B, line 3	2	
3	Total taxable gifts. Add lines 1 and 2	3	
4	Tax computed on amount on line 3 (see *Table for Computing Gift Tax* in instructions)	4	
5	Tax computed on amount on line 2 (see *Table for Computing Gift Tax* in instructions)	5	
6	Balance. Subtract line 5 from line 4	6	
7	Applicable credit amount. If donor has DSUE amount from predeceased spouse(s) or Restored Exclusion Amount, enter amount from Schedule C, line 5; otherwise, see instructions	7	
8	Enter the applicable credit against tax allowable for all prior periods (from Sch. B, line 1, col. C)	8	
9	Balance. Subtract line 8 from line 7. Do not enter less than zero	9	
10	Enter 20% (0.20) of the amount allowed as a specific exemption for gifts made after September 8, 1976, and before January 1, 1977. See instructions	10	
11	Balance. Subtract line 10 from line 9. Do not enter less than zero	11	
12	Applicable credit. Enter the smaller of line 6 or line 11	12	
13	Credit for foreign gift taxes (see instructions)	13	
14	Total credits. Add lines 12 and 13	14	
15	Balance. Subtract line 14 from line 6. Do not enter less than zero	15	
16	Generation-skipping transfer taxes (from Schedule D, Part 3, col. G, total)	16	
17	Total tax. Add lines 15 and 16	17	
18	Gift and generation-skipping transfer taxes prepaid with extension of time to file	18	
19	If line 18 is less than line 17, enter **balance due.** See instructions	19	
20	If line 18 is greater than line 17, enter **amount to be refunded**	20	

Sign Here

Under penalties of perjury, I declare that I have examined this return, including any accompanying schedules and statements, and to the best of my knowledge and belief, it is true, correct, and complete. Declaration of preparer (other than donor) is based on all information of which preparer has any knowledge.

May the IRS discuss this return with the preparer shown below? See instructions. ☐ Yes ☐ No

▶   Signature of donor   Date

Paid Preparer Use Only

Print/Type preparer's name	Preparer's signature	Date	Check ☐ if self-employed	PTIN
Firm's name ▶			Firm's EIN ▶	
Firm's address ▶			Phone no.	

Attach check or money order here.

For Disclosure, Privacy Act, and Paperwork Reduction Act Notice, see the instructions for this form.   Cat. No. 16783M   Form **709** (2021)

SCHEDULE A   **Computation of Taxable Gifts** (Including transfers in trust) (see instructions)

A   Does the value of any item listed on Schedule A reflect any valuation discount? If "Yes," attach explanation . . . . Yes ☐   No ☐

B   ☐ ◄ Check here if you elect under section 529(c)(2)(B) to treat any contributions made this year to a qualified tuition program as made ratably over a 5-year period beginning this year. See instructions. Attach explanation.

Part 1—Gifts Subject Only to Gift Tax. Gifts less political organization, medical, and educational exclusions. See instructions.

A Item number	B • Donee's name and address • Relationship to donor (if any) • Description of gift • If the gift was of securities, give CUSIP no. • If closely held entity, give EIN	C	D Donor's adjusted basis of gift	E Date of gift	F Value at date of gift	G For split gifts, enter ½ of column F	H Net transfer (subtract col. G from col. F)
1							

*Gifts made by spouse—complete **only** if you are splitting gifts with your spouse and he/she also made gifts.*

Total of Part 1. Add amounts from Part 1, column H . . . . ► | | |

Part 2—Direct Skips. Gifts that are direct skips and are subject to both gift tax and generation-skipping transfer tax. You must list the gifts in chronological order.

A Item number	B • Donee's name and address • Relationship to donor (if any) • Description of gift • If the gift was of securities, give CUSIP no. • If closely held entity, give EIN	C 2632(b) election out	D Donor's adjusted basis of gift	E Date of gift	F Value at date of gift	G For split gifts, enter ½ of column F	H Net transfer (subtract col. G from col. F)
1							

*Gifts made by spouse—complete **only** if you are splitting gifts with your spouse and he/she also made gifts.*

Total of Part 2. Add amounts from Part 2, column H . . . . ► | | |

Part 3—Indirect Skips and Other Transfers in Trust. Gifts to trusts that are indirect skips as defined under section 2632(c) or to trusts that are currently subject to gift tax and may later be subject to generation-skipping transfer tax. You must list these gifts in chronological order.

A Item number	B • Donee's name and address • Relationship to donor (if any) • Description of gift • If the gift was of securities, give CUSIP no. • If closely held entity, give EIN	C 2632(c) election	D Donor's adjusted basis of gift	E Date of gift	F Value at date of gift	G For split gifts, enter ½ of column F	H Net transfer (subtract col. G from col. F)
1							

*Gifts made by spouse—complete **only** if you are splitting gifts with your spouse and he/she also made gifts.*

Total of Part 3. Add amounts from Part 3, column H . . . . ► | | |

(If more space is needed, attach additional statements.)

Part 4—Taxable Gift Reconciliation

1	Total value of gifts of donor. Add totals from column H of Parts 1, 2, and 3	1	
2	Total annual exclusions for gifts listed on line 1 (see instructions)	2	
3	Total included amount of gifts. Subtract line 2 from line 1	3	

Deductions (see instructions)

4	Gifts of interests to spouse for which a marital deduction will be claimed, based on item numbers _____ of Schedule A	4		
5	Exclusions attributable to gifts on line 4	5		
6	Marital deduction. Subtract line 5 from line 4	6		
7	Charitable deduction, based on item numbers _____ less exclusions	7		
8	Total deductions. Add lines 6 and 7		8	
9	Subtract line 8 from line 3		9	
10	Generation-skipping transfer taxes payable with this Form 709 (from Schedule D, Part 3, col. G, total)		10	
11	**Taxable gifts.** Add lines 9 and 10. Enter here and on page 1, Part 2—Tax Computation, line 1		11	

Terminable Interest (QTIP) Marital Deduction. (See instructions for Schedule A, Part 4, line 4.)

If a trust (or other property) meets the requirements of qualified terminable interest property under section 2523(f), and:

    a. The trust (or other property) is listed on Schedule A; and

    b. The value of the trust (or other property) is entered in whole or in part as a deduction on Schedule A, Part 4, line 4, then the donor shall be deemed to have made an election to have such trust (or other property) treated as qualified terminable interest property under section 2523(f).

If less than the entire value of the trust (or other property) that the donor has included in Parts 1 and 3 of Schedule A is entered as a deduction on line 4, the donor shall be considered to have made an election only as to a fraction of the trust (or other property). The numerator of this fraction is equal to the amount of the trust (or other property) deducted on Schedule A, Part 4, line 6. The denominator is equal to the total value of the trust (or other property) listed in Parts 1 and 3 of Schedule A.

If you make the QTIP election, the terminable interest property involved will be included in your spouse's gross estate upon his or her death (section 2044). See instructions for line 4 of Schedule A. If your spouse disposes (by gift or otherwise) of all or part of the qualifying life income interest, he or she will be considered to have made a transfer of the entire property that is subject to the gift tax. See *Transfer of Certain Life Estates Received From Spouse* in the instructions.

12   **Election Out of QTIP Treatment of Annuities**

    ☐ ◀ Check here if you elect under section 2523(f)(6) **not** to treat as qualified terminable interest property any joint and survivor annuities that are reported on Schedule A and would otherwise be treated as qualified terminable interest property under section 2523(f). See instructions. Enter the item numbers from Schedule A for the annuities for which you are making this election ▶

SCHEDULE B   **Gifts From Prior Periods**

If you answered "Yes" on line 11a of page 1, Part 1, see the instructions for completing Schedule B. If you answered "No," skip to the Tax Computation on page 1 (or Schedule C or D, if applicable). Complete Schedule A before beginning Schedule B. See instructions for recalculation of the column C amounts. Attach calculations.

A Calendar year or calendar quarter (see instructions)	B Internal Revenue office where prior return was filed	C Amount of applicable credit (unified credit) against gift tax for periods after December 31, 1976	D Amount of specific exemption for prior periods ending before January 1, 1977	E Amount of taxable gifts

1	Totals for prior periods	1			
2	Amount, if any, by which total specific exemption, line 1, column D, is more than $30,000			2	
3	Total amount of taxable gifts for prior periods. Add amount on line 1, column E, and amount, if any, on line 2. Enter here and on page 1, Part 2—Tax Computation, line 2			3	

(If more space is needed, attach additional statements.)   Form **709** (2021)

SCHEDULE C   Deceased Spousal Unused Exclusion (DSUE) Amount and Restored Exclusion

Provide the following information to determine the DSUE amount and applicable credit received from prior spouses. Complete Schedule A before beginning Schedule C.

A Name of deceased spouse (dates of death after December 31, 2010, only)	B Date of death	C Portability election made?		D If "Yes," DSUE amount received from spouse	E DSUE amount applied by donor to lifetime gifts (list current and prior gifts)	F Date of gift(s) (enter as mm/dd/yy for Part 1 and as yyyy for Part 2)
		Yes	No			
Part 1—DSUE RECEIVED FROM LAST DECEASED SPOUSE						
Part 2—DSUE RECEIVED FROM PREDECEASED SPOUSE(S)						

TOTAL (for all DSUE amounts applied from column E for Part 1 and Part 2) . . . . ▶

1	Donor's basic exclusion amount (see instructions)	**1**
2	Total from column E, Parts 1 and 2	**2**
3	Restored Exclusion Amount (see instructions)	**3**
4	Add lines 1, 2, and 3	**4**
5	Applicable credit on amount in line 4 (see *Table for Computing Gift Tax* in the instructions). Enter here and on line 7, Part 2—Tax Computation	**5**

SCHEDULE D   Computation of Generation-Skipping Transfer Tax

Note: Inter vivos direct skips that are completely excluded by the GST exemption must still be fully reported (including value and exemptions claimed) on Schedule D.

Part 1—Generation-Skipping Transfers. List items from Schedule A first, then items to be reported on Schedule D, including any transfers subject to an Estate Tax Inclusion Period (ETIP).

A Item number (from Schedule A, Part 2, col. A, then ETIP transfers, if any)	B Description (only for ETIP transfers)	C Value (from Schedule A, Part 2, col. H, or close of ETIP described in col. B)	D Nontaxable portion of transfer	E Net transfer (subtract col. D from col. C)
1				
Gifts made by spouse (for gift splitting only)				

(If more space is needed, attach additional statements.)

Form **709** (2021)

Part 2—GST Exemption Reconciliation (Section 2631) and Section 2652(a)(3) Election

Check here ▶ ☐ if you are making a section 2652(a)(3) (special QTIP) election. See instructions.

Enter the item numbers from Schedule A of the gifts for which you are making this election ▶ ....

1	Maximum allowable exemption (see instructions)	1
2	Total exemption used for periods before filing this return	2
3	Exemption available for this return. Subtract line 2 from line 1	3
4	Exemption claimed on this return from Part 3, column C, total below	4
5	Automatic allocation of exemption to transfers reported on Schedule A, Part 3. To opt out of the automatic allocation rules, you must attach an "**Election Out**" statement. See instructions	5
6	Exemption allocated to transfers not shown on line 4 or line 5 above. **You must attach a "Notice of Allocation."** See instructions	6
7	Add lines 4, 5, and 6	7
8	Exemption available for future transfers. Subtract line 7 from line 3	8

Part 3—Tax Computation

A Item number (from Schedule D, Part 1)	B Net transfer (from Schedule D, Part 1, col. E)	C GST exemption allocated	D Divide col. C by col. B	E Inclusion ratio (Subtract col. D from 1.000)	F Applicable rate (multiply col. E by 40% (0.40))	G Generation-skipping transfer tax (multiply col. B by col. F)
1						
Gifts made by spouse (for gift splitting only)						
Total exemption claimed. Enter here and on Part 2, line 4, above. May not exceed Part 2, line 3, above . . .			**Total generation-skipping transfer tax.** Enter here; on page 3, Schedule A, Part 4, line 10; and on page 1, Part 2—Tax Computation, line 16			

(If more space is needed, attach additional statements.)

SOCIAL SECURITY NUMBERS

PERSON   ### NUMBER

1. _____   _____

2. _____   _____

3. _____   _____

4. _____   _____

5. _____   _____

6. _____   _____

MY ACCOUNTANT

ACCOUNTANT: _____

_____

MY PREVIOUS TAX RETURNS

	YEAR	LOCATION
PREVIOUS YEARS:	_____	_____
	_____	_____
	_____	_____

LOCATION,

CURRENT-YEAR'S

(INCOMPLETE)

INFORMATION: _____   _____

CHECKING ACCOUNTS

1.ISSUER: _____

LOCATION ACCOUNT: _____

_____

ACCOUNT NUMBER: _____

ROUTING NUMBER: _____

ID: _____

PASSWORD: _____

TO FIND ON INTERNET: _____

2. ISSUER: _____

LOCATION CCOUNT: _____

_____

ACCOUNT NUMBER: _____

ROUTING NUMBER: _____

ID: _____

PASSWORD: _____

TO FIND ON INTERNET: _____

FINANCIAL ADVISOR

FINANCIAL ADVISOR: _____

_____

TEL.: _____

ADDRESS: _____

_____

_____

FINANCIAL ASSETS

TRUST:

TITLE: _____

LOCATION: _____

TRUSTEE: _____

_____

BROKER: _____

_____

TEL.: _____

ROTH IRA:

TITLE: _____

LOCATION: _____

BROKER: _____

_____

TEL: _____

TRADITIONAL IRA:

TITLE: _____

LOCATION: _____

BROKER: _____

TEL: _____

BROKERAGE ACCOUNT

TITLE: _____

LOCATION: _____

BROKER: _____

TEL.: _____

PENSION:

1.COMPANY: _____

EFFECTIVE YET?: _____

INCOME: _____

TERMS: _____

_____

2.COMPANY: _____

EFFECTIVE YET?_____

INCOME: _____

TERMS: _____

PROFIT-SHARING PLAN:

1.COMPANY: _____

EFFECTIVE YET? _____

INCOME: _____

TERMS: _____

_____

2.COMPANY: _____

EFFECTIVE YET? _____

INCOME: _____

TERMS: _____

OTHER: _____

LOCATION: _____

CONTACT: _____

TEL.: _____

ANNUITIES

1. INSURER: _____

CONTACT: _____

TYPE: _____

MY STATUS—

ANNUITANT/OWNER: _____

DEATH BENEFIT

PROVISION? _____

BENEFICIARIES: 1. _____

_____

2. _____

_____

3._____

_____

4._____

_____

5._____

2.INSURER: _____

CONTACT: _____

TYPE: _____

MY STATUS--

ANNUITANT/OWNER:_____

DEATH BENEFIT

PROVISION?: _____

BEFICIARIES: 1._____

_____

2._____

_____

3._____

_____

4._____

_____

3.INSURER: _____

CONTACT: _____

TYPE: _____

MY STATUS—

ANNUITANT/OWNER: _____

DEATH BENEFIT

PROVISION? _____

BENEFICIARIES:1. _____

—

_____

2._____

_____

3._____

_____

4._____

_____

<u>REVERSE MORTGAGE</u>

LENDER: _____

PROPERTY

ADDRESS: _____

_____

CONTACT: _____

_____

LOAN AMOUNT: _____

INTEREST RATE: _____

ACCUMULATED

INTEREST: _____

TERMS FOR NON-

BROWING SPOUSE:_____

_____

_____

PARTNERSHIPS

1.TITLE: _____

LOCATION: _____

PARTNER: _____

TEL: _____

2.TITLE: _____

LOCATION: _____

PARTNER: _____

TEL: _____

PATENTS

1.TITLE: _____

LOCATION: _____

DESCRIPTION: _____

_____

2.TITLE: _____

LOCATION: _____

DESCRIPTION: _____

_____

<u>COPYRIGHTS</u>

1.TITLE: _____

LOCATION: _____

_____

DESCRIPTION:_____

_____

2.TITLE: _____

LOCATION: _____

_____

DESCRIPTION: _____

_____

CREDIT/ DEBIT CARDS

BANK DEBIT CARD:_____

THIS CARD IS IMPORTANT AS IT CONSTITUTES THE

ACCESS TO YOUR BANK ACCOUNT AND TO ATMs

1.ISSUER: _____

NUMBER: _____

EXPIRATION DATE: _____

SECURITY CODE: _____

2.ISSUER: _____

NUMBER: _____

EXPIRATION DATE: _____

SECURITY CODE: _____

3.ISSUER: _____

NUMBER: _____

EXPIRATION DATE: _____

SECURITY CODE: _____

4.ISSUER:_____

NUMBER: _____

EXPIRATION DATE: _____

SECURITY CODE: _____

LIFE INSURANCE

1.AGENT/BROKER: _____

TEL.: _____

CARRIER: _____

POLICY NUMBER: _____

TYPE: _____

VALUE: _____

2.AGENT/BROKER: _____

TEL.:   _____

CARRIER: _____

POLICY NUMBER: _____

TYPE: _____

VALUE: _____

3.AGENT/BROKER:_____

TEL.:   _____

CARRIER: _____

POLICY NUMBER:_____

TYPE: _____

VALUE: _____

4.AGENT/BROKER: _____

TEL.: _____

CARRIER: _____

POLICY NUMBER: _____

TYPE: _____

VALUE: _____

REAL ESTATE

OWNER(S): _____

ADDRESS: _____

DATE ACQUIRED: _____

ORIGINAL COST: _____

BASIS UPDATED: _____

DEED LOCATION: _____

TITLE INSURANCE

COMPANY: _____

POLICY
LOCATION: _____

MORTGAGE

LENDER: _____

OUTSTANDING

DEBT: _____

REAL ESTATE

AGENT: _____

2 . DESCRIPTION: _____

OWNER(S): _____

ADDRESS: _____

_____

DATE ACQUIRED: _____

ORIGINAL COST: _____

BASIS UPDATED: _____

DEED LOCATION: _____

TITLE INSURANCE

  COMPANY: _____

POLICY LOCATION: _____

MORTGAGE

LENDER: _____

OUTSTANDING

  DEBT: _____

REAL ESTATE

AGENT: _____

3.DESCRIPTION: _____

_____

OWNER(S): _____

_____

ADDRESS: _____

DATE ACQUIRED: _____

ORIGINAL COST: _____

BASIS UPDATED: _____

DEED LOCATION: _____

TITLE INSURANCE

COMPANY: _____

POLICY LOCATION: _____

MORTGAGE

LENDER: _____

OUTSTANDING

DEBT: _____

REAL ESTATE

AGENT: _____

HOMEOWNERS' INSURANCE

INSURER: _____

POLICY NUMBER: _____

POLICY LOCATION: _____

COVERAGE: _____

_____

_____

RENTERS' INSURANCE

INSURER: _____

POLICY NUMBER: _____

POLICY LOCATION: _____

COVERAGE: _____

_____

AUTOMOBILES

1.MAKE: _____

VIN: _____

MODEL: _____

YEAR: _____

TITLE: _____

LOAN: _____

REGISTRATION/
SERVICE: _____

INSURANCE POLICY: _____

2.MAKE: _____

VIN: _____

MODEL: _____

YEAR: _____

TITLE: _____

LOAN: _____

REGISTRATION/

SERVICE: _____

INSURANCE POLICY: _____

3. MAKE: _____

VIN: _____

MODEL: _____

YEAR: _____

TITLE: _____

LOAN: _____

REGISTRATION/
SERVICE: _____

INSURANCE POLICY: _____

AUTOMOBILE INSURANCE

1. CAR COVERED: _____

OWNER(S): _____

_____

VIN: _____

INSURER: _____

TITLE: _____

POLICY NUMBER: _____

COVERAGE: _____

2.CAR COVERED: _____

OWNER(S): _____

_____

VIN: _____

INSURER: _____

TITLE: _____

POLICY NUMBER: _____

COVERAGE: _____

3.CAR COVERED:_____

OWNER(S):_____

_____

VIN:_____

INSURER:_____

TITLE:_____

POLICY NUMBER:_____

COVERAGE:_____

PERSONAL PROPERTY INSURANCE

SPECIAL ITEMS:

1.DESCRIPTION: _____

VALUE: _____

INSURER: _____

POLICY NUMBER: _____

2. DESCRIPTION: _____

VALUE: _____

INSURER: _____

POLICY NUMBER: _____

3. DESCRIPTION: _____

VALUE: _____

INSURER: _____

POLICY NUMBER: _____

4.DESCRIPTION: _____

VALUE: _____

INSURER: _____

POLICY NUMBER: _____

<u>UMBRELLA POLICY</u>

CARRIER: _____

COVERAGE: _____

_____

BODILY INJURY: _____

PROPERTY DAMAGE:_____

OR **COMBINED:** _____

HEALTH INSURANCE

1. CARRIER: _____

TEL: _____

POLICY NO.: _____

COVERAGE: _____

_____

2. CARRIER: _____

TEL.: _____

POLICY NO.: _____

COVERAGE: _____

MEDICARE

ID NUMBER: _____

CARD LOCATION: _____

MEDICARE SUPPLEMENT
(MEDIGAP)

CARRIER: _____

TEL.: _____

PLAN NUMBER: _____

COVERAGE: _____

_____

MEDICARE ADVANTAGE
(PART C)

CARRIER: _____

TEL.: _____

PLAN NUMBER: _____

CARD LOCATION: _____

COVERAGE: _____

_____

LONG-TERM CARE

CARRIER: _____

AGENT: _____

COVERAGE: _____

**FACILITY
LOCATION:** _____

_____

OTHER INSURANCE

1.TYPE: _____

CARRIER: _____

PLAN NUMBER: _____

CARD LOCATION: _____

COVERAGE: _____

_____

2.TYPE: _____

CARRIER: _____

PLAN NUMBER: _____

CARD LOCATION: _____

COVERAGE: _____

_____

COMPUTER

ACCESS ID: _____

PASSWORD: _____

DIRECTIONS

TO OPEN: _____

_____

EMAIL ADDRESS: _____

<u>PASSWORDS</u>

IMPORTANT PASSWORDS:

1. _____   _____

2. _____   _____

3. _____   _____

4. _____   _____

5. _____   _____

6. _____   _____

7._____   _____

8 . _____ _____

9. _____ _____

10._____ _____

<u>KEYS</u>

KEY 1. _____ _____

KEY 2. _____ _____

KEY 3. _____ _____

KEY 4. _____ _____

KEY 5. _____ _____

KEY 6. _____ _____

KEY 7. _____ _____

KEY 8. _____ _____

KEY LOCATION, CARS:

1. _____   _____

2. _____   _____

3. _____   _____

KEY LOCATION, HOUSE

1. _____   _____

2. _____   _____

3. _____   _____

SAFE DEPOSIT BOX

OWNERSHIP: _____

_____

LOCATION: _____

COMBINATION: **LEFT:** _____

RIGHT: _____

LEFT: _____

RIGHT: _____

_OR_ KEY: _____

HOUSE SAFES

1._____

COMBINATION:

    LEFT: _____

    RIGHT: _____

    LEFT: _____

    RIGHT: _____

IDIOSYNCRACIES: _____

_____

2. _____

COMBINATION:

     LEFT: _____

     RIGHT: _____

     LEFT: _____

     RIGHT: _____

IDIOSYNCRACIES: _____

_____

_____

SAFE WITH KEY:

                    KEY'S LOCATION: _____

                    IDIOSYNCRACIES:

_____

_____

<u>GOLD</u>

SPECIAL ITEMS:

1. DESCRIPTION: _____

LOCATION: _____

COST: _____

CURRENT

VALUE: _____

2.DESCRIPTION: _____

LOCATION: _____

COST: _____

CURRENT VALUE: _____

3. DESCRIPTION: _____

LOCATION: _____

COST: _____

CURRENT VALUE: _____

4. DESCRIPTION: _____

LOCATION: _____

COST: _____

CURRENT VALUE: _____

5. DESCRIPTION: _____

LOCATION: _____

COST: _____

CURRENT VALUE: _____

SILVER

SPECIAL ITEMS:

1.DESCRIPTION: _____

LOCATION: _____

DATE
ACQUIRED: _____

SILVERSMITH: _____

COST: _____

CURRENT VALUE: _____

INSURANCE: _____

2.DESCRIPTION: _____

LOCATION: _____

DATE
ACQUIRED: _____

SILVERSMITH: _____

COST: _____

CURRENT VALUE: _____

INSURANCE: _____

3.DESCRIPTION: _____

LOCATION: _____

DATE
ACQUIRED: _____

SILVERSMITH: _____

COST: _____

CURRENT VALUE _____

INSURANCE: _____

4.DESCRIPTION: _____

LOCATION: _____

DATE

ACQUIRED: _____

SILVERSMITH: _____

COST: _____

CURRENT

VALUE: _____

INSURANCE: _____

ANTIQUES

SPECIAL PIECES:

1. DESCRIPTION: _____

LOCATION: _____

DATE
ACQUIRED: _____

COST: _____

CURRENT
VALUE: _____

INSURANCE: _____

2. DESCRIPTION: _____

LOCATION: _____

**DATE
ACQUIRED:** _____

COST: _____

**CURRENT
VALUE:** _____

INSURANCE: _____

3.DESCRIPTION: _____

LOCATION: _____

DATE
ACQUIRED: _____

COST: _____

CURRENT
VALUE: _____

INSURANCE: _____

4.DESCRIPTION: _____

LOCATION: _____

DATE

ACQUIRED: _____

COST: _____

CURRENT

VALUE: _____

INSURANCE: _____

5. DESCRIPTION: _____

LOCATION: _____

DATE
ACQUIRED: _____

COST: _____

CURRENT
VALUE: _____

INSURANCE: _____

PAINTINGS

1. DESCRIPTION: _____

_____

ARTIST: _____

DATE

ACQUIRED: _____

COST: _____

CURRENT

VALUE: _____

INSURANCE: _____

2. DESCRIPTION: _____

_____

ARTIST: _____

DATE
ACQUIRED: _____

COST: _____

CURRENT
VALUE: _____

INSURANCE: _____

3.DESCRIPTION: _____

_____

ARTIST: _____

DATE
ACQUIRED: _____

COST: _____

CURRENT
VALUE: _____

INSURANCE: _____

4.DESCRIPTION: _____

ARTIST: _____

DATE
ACQUIRED: _____

COST: _____

CURRENT
VALUE: _____

INSURANCE: _____

5. DESCRIPTION: _____

ARTIST: _____

DATE
ACQUIRED: _____

COST: _____

CURRENT
VALUE: _____

INSURANCE: _____

<u>STAMP COLLECTION</u>

LOCATION: _____

_____

SPECIAL ITEMS:

1. _____

2. _____

3. _____

4. _____

5. _____

6. _____

CLUBS

1. CLUB NAME: _____

ADDRESS: _____

MY MEMBERSHIP
NUMBER: _____

MEMBERSHIP
CATEGORY: _____

DATE JOINED: _____

2.CLUB NAME: _____

ADDRESS: _____

MY MEMBERSHIP

NUMBER: _____

MEMBERSHIP

CATEGORY: _____

DATE JOINED: _____

3.CLUB NAME: _____

ADDRESS: _____

MY MEMBERSHIP

 NUMBER: _____

MEMBERSHIP

CATEGORY: _____

DATE JOINED: _____

4.CLUB NAME: _____

ADDRESS: _____

MY MEMBERSHIP

NUMBER: _____

MEMBERSHIP

CATEGORY: _____

DATE JOINED: _____

GIFTS TO CHARITABLE INSTITUTIONS

1.CHARITABLE

REMAINDER

TRUST: _____

IN NAME OF: _____

RECIPIENT CHARITY: _____

CONTRIBUTION FORM,

CASH/SECURITIES/OTHER: _____

COST BASIS: _____

INCOME TO ME: _____

TERMS: _____

_____

2.CHARITABLE
GIFT ANNUITY: _____

IN NAME OF: _____

RECIPIENTCHARITY: _____

CONTRIBUTION,
CASH/SECURITIES/OTHER:_____

COST BASIS: _____

INCOME TO ME: _____

TRUSTEE: _____

_____

3. OTHER TYPE

CONTRIBUTION: _____

IN NAME OF: _____

CHARITY: _____

CONTRIBUTION,
CASH/SECURITIES/OTHER: _____

COST BASIS: _____

TRUSTEEE: _____

INCOME TO ME: _____

TERMS: _____

_____

PROFESSIONAL COMMITMENTS

1._____

     POSITION: _____

2._____

     POSITION: _____

3._____

     POSITION: _____

CORPORATE BOARDS:

1._____

        POSITION:_____

2._____

        POSITION:_____

3._____

        POSITION:_____

<u>VOLUNTEER COMMITMENTS</u>

1._____

     POSITION: _____

2._____

     POSITION: _____

3._____

     POSITION: _____

MY OTHER RESPONSIBILITIES

EXECUTOR: _____

_____

CONSERVATOR: _____

_____

OTHER: _____

_____

<u>FRIENDS</u>

1. _____TEL./EMAIL:_____

2._____ TEL./EMAIL: _____

3._____TEL./EMAIL: _____

4. _____TEL./EMAIL: _____

5._____TEL./EMAIL: _____

6._____TEL./EMAIL: _____

7._____TEL./EMAIL: _____

8. _____TEL./EMAIL: _____

9._____TEL./EMAIL: _____

10._____TEL./EMAIL: _____

PERSONS TO CONTACT

1._____TEL./EMAIL: _____

2._____TEL./EMAIL: _____

3. _____ TEL./EMAIL: _____

4. _____TEL./EMAIL: _____

5._____TEL./EMAIL: _____

6. _____TEL./EMAIL: _____

7._____TEL./EMAIL: _____

8. _____TEL./EMAIL: _____

9._____TEL./EMAIL: _____

10._____TEL./EMAIL: _____

DOCTORS

INTERNIST: _____

_____

OPTHALMOLOGIST: _____

_____

CARDIOLOGIST: _____

_____

ONCOLOGIST: _____

_____

RHUMATOLOGIST: _____

_____

DERMATOLOGIST: _____

_____

DENTIST: _____

_____

VETERINARIAN: _____

_____

OTHER: _____

_____

HOUSE MAINTENANCE

ELECTRICIAN: _____

_____

FURNACE: _____

_____

IRRIGATION: _____

_____

LAWN/SNOW: _____

_____

CARPENTER: _____

_____

SECURITY: _____

_____

PLUMBER: _____

_____

PAINTER: _____

_____

OTHER: _____

_____

THE END,

almost

Dear Executor,

I have now come to the end of this workbook with hopes that my efforts will help make your job easier and more accurate than it might have been. May you find that I have left you sufficient information to accurately complete Probate and Form 706 and to settle the rest of my estate.

I add my thanks for making my family's life more peaceful and settlement more accurate than it might have been.

With best regards,

_____

NAME

_____

DATE

PART II

Now that you (writer) have completed your task, at least for the present, please let me (MJAJ) add a few words:

Part II is for your information, sketching out what may happen to your estate after your death. It is a different animal from Part I because you were around to fill in the pertinent information for Part I, whereas in Part II the Probate and Form 706 phases have to be completed by someone else.

Part II here very briefly covers 1) the IRS Form 709, the United States Gift (and Generation-Skipping Transfer) Tax Return, which you already know about, and 2) Probate and 3) the IRS Form 706, the United States Estate (and Generation-Skipping Transfer) Tax Return, which your estate will deal with.

I have listed Form 709 first, then the Probate Court secondly, and finally Form 706 thirdly because of their chronology in your situation.

FORM 709

Hopefully, your executor should find most of the information required for Form 709 in Part I. It covers gifts and generation-skipping transfers.

Taxable gifts for 2019 and 2020 are those in general in excess of $15,000, the annual gift exclusion, made to persons other than your spouse, and excluding most gifts made to political organizations and expenses covering medical and educational costs of others. The amount rises to $16,000 for 2022.

Generation Skipping Transfers are another category needing to be reported here.

SEE PREVIOUS PAGES IN PART I REGARDING

IRS FORM 709

PROBATE

Probate is the function of the 50 states and the District of Columbia. Therefore, there naturally are many variables. Some states have a Probate Court; others handle estates through a Superior Court, District Court, Court of Chancery, Family Court, Circuit Court or a number of other courts.

Presumably you have already appointed your executor and discussed your wishes for your estate with him or her. After your death, your executor will submit your will to Probate for validation. The court will then formally appoint your executor. If you have not left a will, the court will appoint an administrator.

It is the duty of the PROBATE to officially notify your heirs and beneficiaries of your death, then to oversee the executor or administrator in the collection of your assets, to see that your taxes and other liabilities are paid, and ultimately to distribute the remaining proceeds to your heirs and beneficiaries. It therefore generally supervises the settling of your estate.

The necessity of going through probate depends on the particular state. Small estates, IRAs, 401(k)s, trusts, pension plans, joint holdings, assets with rights of survivorship, and certain joint holdings are not always required to go through the probate process, but it depends on the State law.

IRS FORM 706

There are many reasons why you should have wanted to compile the information into DEAR EXECUTOR: A WORKBOOK, but the number of estates that will actually file Form 706, the Estate Tax Return, might surprise you.

The number of estates required to file and pay U.S. estate taxes has declined drastically in the past two decades, until for deaths in 2020 the estimated estate tax returns to be filed for those dying in that year is estimated at 4,100 and of those only 1,900 are expected to pay tax.[1] The main reason for the decline is that the exemption has now increased to $11, 600,000 of taxable estate for the year 2022, whereas as recently as the year 2001 it had been $675,000. Because of our deficit situation today, a decrease in the exemption in the not-too-distant future would not be a surprise.

For your interest, I have attached a copy of IRS Form 706; there is not yet a specifically 2021 version.

---

[1] The Tax Policy Center's Briefing Book, "Key Elements of the U.S. Tax System." No page numbers or date of publication.

Form **706**
(Rev. August 2019)

Department of the Treasury
Internal Revenue Service

United States Estate (and Generation-Skipping Transfer) Tax Return

▶ Estate of a citizen or resident of the United States (see instructions). To be filed for decedents dying after December 31, 2018.
▶ Go to *www.irs.gov/Form706* for instructions and the latest information.

OMB No. 1545-0015

Part 1—Decedent and Executor

1a Decedent's first name and middle initial (and maiden name, if any)	1b Decedent's last name	2 Decedent's social security no.

3a City, town, or post office; county; state or province; country; and ZIP or foreign postal code	3b Year domicile established	4 Date of birth	5 Date of death

6b Executor's address (number and street including apartment or suite no.; city, town, or post office; state or province; country; and ZIP or foreign postal code) and phone no.

6a Name of executor (see instructions)

6c Executor's social security number (see instructions)

Phone no.

6d If there are multiple executors, check here ☐ and attach a list showing the names, addresses, telephone numbers, and SSNs of the additional executors.

7a Name and location of court where will was probated or estate administered	7b Case number

8 If decedent died testate, check here ▶ ☐ and attach a certified copy of the will.   9 If you extended the time to file this Form 706, check here ▶ ☐

10 If Schedule R-1 is attached, check here ▶ ☐   11 If you are estimating the value of assets included in the gross estate on line 1 pursuant to the special rule of Reg. section 20.2010-2(a)(7)(ii), check here ▶ ☐

Part 2—Tax Computation

1	Total gross estate less exclusion (from Part 5—Recapitulation, item 13)	1	
2	Tentative total allowable deductions (from Part 5—Recapitulation, item 24)	2	
3a	Tentative taxable estate (subtract line 2 from line 1)	3a	
b	State death tax deduction	3b	
c	Taxable estate (subtract line 3b from line 3a)	3c	
4	Adjusted taxable gifts (see instructions)	4	
5	Add lines 3c and 4	5	
6	Tentative tax on the amount on line 5 from Table A in the instructions	6	
7	Total gift tax paid or payable (see instructions)	7	
8	Gross estate tax (subtract line 7 from line 6)	8	

9a	Basic exclusion amount	9a		
b	Deceased spousal unused exclusion (DSUE) amount from predeceased spouse(s), if any (from Section D, Part 6—Portability of Deceased Spousal Unused Exclusion)	9b		
c	Restored exclusion amount (see instructions)	9c		
d	Applicable exclusion amount (add lines 9a, 9b, and 9c)	9d		
e	Applicable credit amount (tentative tax on the amount in line 9d from Table A in the instructions)	9e		
10	Adjustment to applicable credit amount (May not exceed $6,000. See instructions.)	10		
11	Allowable applicable credit amount (subtract line 10 from line 9e)		11	
12	Subtract line 11 from line 8 (but do not enter less than zero)		12	
13	Credit for foreign death taxes (from Schedule P). (Attach Form(s) 706-CE.)	13		
14	Credit for tax on prior transfers (from Schedule Q)	14		
15	Total credits (add lines 13 and 14)		15	
16	Net estate tax (subtract line 15 from line 12)		16	
17	Generation-skipping transfer (GST) taxes payable (from Schedule R, Part 2, line 10)		17	
18	Total transfer taxes (add lines 16 and 17)		18	
19	Prior payments (explain in an attached statement)		19	
20	Balance due (or overpayment) (subtract line 19 from line 18)		20	

Under penalties of perjury, I declare that I have examined this return, including accompanying schedules and statements, and to the best of my knowledge and belief, it is true, correct, and complete. Declaration of preparer (other than the executor) is based on all information of which preparer has any knowledge.

Sign Here

Signature of executor _____ Date _____

Signature of executor _____ Date _____

Paid Preparer Use Only

Print/Type preparer's name	Preparer's signature	Date	Check ☐ if self-employed	PTIN
Firm's name ▶			Firm's EIN ▶	
Firm's address ▶			Phone no.	

For Privacy Act and Paperwork Reduction Act Notice, see instructions.   Cat. No. 20548R   Form **706** (Rev. 8-2019)

Form 706 (Rev. 8-2019)

	Decedent's social security number

Estate of:

Part 3—Elections by the Executor

Note: For information on electing portability of the decedent's DSUE amount, including how to opt out of the election, see Part 6—Portability of Deceased Spousal Unused Exclusion.

Note: Some of the following elections may require the posting of bonds or liens.

			Yes	No
	Please check "Yes" or "No" for each question. See instructions.			
1	Do you elect alternate valuation?	**1**		
2	Do you elect special-use valuation? If "Yes," you must complete and attach Schedule A-1	**2**		
3	Do you elect to pay the taxes in installments as described in section 6166? . . . . If "Yes," you must attach the additional information described in the instructions. **Note: By electing section 6166 installment payments, you may be required to provide security for estate tax deferred under section 6166 and interest in the form of a surety bond or a section 6324A lien.**	**3**		
4	Do you elect to postpone the part of the taxes due to a reversionary or remainder interest as described in section 6163? .	**4**		

Part 4—General Information

Note: Please attach the necessary supplemental documents. **You must attach the death certificate.** See instructions.

Authorization to receive confidential tax information under Reg. section 601.504(b)(2)(i); to act as the estate's representative before the IRS; and to make written or oral presentations on behalf of the estate:

Name of representative (print or type)	State	Address (number, street, and room or suite no., city, state, and ZIP code)

I declare that I am the ☐ attorney/ ☐ certified public accountant/ ☐ enrolled agent (check the applicable box) for the executor. I am not under suspension or disbarment from practice before the Internal Revenue Service and am qualified to practice in the state shown above.

Signature	CAF number	Date	Telephone number

1   Death certificate number and issuing authority (attach a copy of the death certificate to this return).

2   Decedent's business or occupation. If retired, check here ▶ ☐ and state decedent's former business or occupation.

3a   Marital status of the decedent at time of death:

     ☐ Married   ☐ Widow/widower   ☐ Single   ☐ Legally separated   ☐ Divorced

3b   For all prior marriages, list the name and SSN of the former spouse, the date the marriage ended, and whether the marriage ended by annulment, divorce, or death. Attach additional statements of the same size if necessary.

4a Surviving spouse's name	**4b** Social security number	**4c** Amount received (see instructions)

5   Individuals (other than the surviving spouse), trusts, or other estates who receive benefits from the estate (do not include charitable beneficiaries shown in Schedule O) (see instructions).

Name of individual, trust, or estate receiving $5,000 or more	Identifying number	Relationship to decedent	Amount (see instructions)

All unascertainable beneficiaries and those who receive less than $5,000 . . . . ▶

Total . . . .

If you answer "Yes" to any of the following questions, you must attach additional information as described.		Yes	No
6	Is the estate filing a protective claim for refund? . . . . If "Yes," complete and attach two copies of Schedule PC for each claim.		
7	Does the gross estate contain any section 2044 property (qualified terminable interest property (QTIP) from a prior gift or estate)? See instructions		
8a	Have federal gift tax returns ever been filed? . . . . If "Yes," attach copies of the returns, if available, and furnish the following information.		
b	Period(s) covered **c** Internal Revenue office(s) where filed		
9a	Was there any insurance on the decedent's life that is not included on the return as part of the gross estate?		
b	Did the decedent own any insurance on the life of another that is not included in the gross estate?		

Page 2

154

Estate of:	Decedent's social security number

Part 4—General Information (continued)

If you answer "Yes" to any of the following questions, you must attach additional information as described.	Yes	No
10 Did the decedent at the time of death own any property as a joint tenant with right of survivorship in which **(a)** one or more of the other joint tenants was someone other than the decedent's spouse, and **(b)** less than the full value of the property is included on the return as part of the gross estate? If "Yes," you must complete and attach Schedule E		
11a Did the decedent, at the time of death, own any interest in a partnership (for example, a family limited partnership), an unincorporated business, or a limited liability company; or own any stock in an inactive or closely held corporation?		
b If "Yes," was the value of **any** interest owned (from above) discounted on this estate tax return? If "Yes," see the instructions on reporting the total accumulated or effective discounts taken on Schedule F or G		
12 Did the decedent make any transfer described in sections 2035, 2036, 2037, or 2038? See instructions. If "Yes," you must complete and attach Schedule G		
13a Were there in existence at the time of the decedent's death any trusts created by the decedent during his or her lifetime?		
b Were there in existence at the time of the decedent's death any trusts not created by the decedent under which the decedent possessed any power, beneficial interest, or trusteeship?		
c Was the decedent receiving income from a trust created after October 22, 1986, by a parent or grandparent?		
If "Yes," was there a GST taxable termination (under section 2612) on the death of the decedent?		
d If there was a GST taxable termination (under section 2612), attach a statement to explain. Provide a copy of the trust or will creating the trust, and give the name, address, and phone number of the current trustee(s).		
e Did the decedent at any time during his or her lifetime transfer or sell an interest in a partnership, limited liability company, or closely held corporation to a trust described in line 13a or 13b?		
If "Yes," provide the EIN for this transferred/sold item. ▶		
14 Did the decedent ever possess, exercise, or release any general power of appointment? If "Yes," you must complete and attach Schedule H		
15 Did the decedent have an interest in or a signature or other authority over a financial account in a foreign country, such as a bank account, securities account, or other financial account?		
16 Was the decedent, immediately before death, receiving an annuity described in the "General" paragraph of the instructions for Schedule I or a private annuity? If "Yes," you must complete and attach Schedule I		
17 Was the decedent ever the beneficiary of a trust for which a deduction was claimed by the estate of a predeceased spouse under section 2056(b)(7) and which is not reported on this return? If "Yes," attach an explanation		

Part 5—Recapitulation.

Note: If estimating the value of one or more assets pursuant to the special rule of Reg. section 20.2010-2(a)(7)(ii), enter on both lines 10 and 23 the amount noted in the instructions for the corresponding range of values. See instructions for details.

Item no.	Gross estate		Alternate value	Value at date of death
1	Schedule A—Real Estate	1		
2	Schedule B—Stocks and Bonds	2		
3	Schedule C—Mortgages, Notes, and Cash	3		
4	Schedule D—Insurance on the Decedent's Life (attach Form(s) 712)	4		
5	Schedule E—Jointly Owned Property (attach Form(s) 712 for life insurance)	5		
6	Schedule F—Other Miscellaneous Property (attach Form(s) 712 for life insurance)	6		
7	Schedule G—Transfers During Decedent's Life (att. Form(s) 712 for life insurance)	7		
8	Schedule H—Powers of Appointment	8		
9	Schedule I—Annuities	9		
10	Estimated value of assets subject to the special rule of Reg. section 20.2010-2(a)(7)(ii)	10		
11	Total gross estate (add items 1 through 10)	11		
12	Schedule U—Qualified Conservation Easement Exclusion	12		
13	Total gross estate less exclusion (subtract item 12 from item 11). Enter here and on line 1 of Part 2—Tax Computation	13		

Item no.	Deductions		Amount
14	Schedule J—Funeral Expenses and Expenses Incurred in Administering Property Subject to Claims	14	
15	Schedule K—Debts of the Decedent	15	
16	Schedule K—Mortgages and Liens	16	
17	Total of items 14 through 16	17	
18	Allowable amount of deductions from item 17 (see the instructions for item 18 of the Recapitulation)	18	
19	Schedule L—Net Losses During Administration	19	
20	Schedule L—Expenses Incurred in Administering Property Not Subject to Claims	20	
21	Schedule M—Bequests, etc., to Surviving Spouse	21	
22	Schedule O—Charitable, Public, and Similar Gifts and Bequests	22	
23	Estimated value of deductible assets subject to the special rule of Reg. section 20.2010-2(a)(7)(ii)	23	
24	Tentative total allowable deductions (add items 18 through 23). Enter here and on line 2 of the Tax Computation	24	

Page 3

	Decedent's social security number
Estate of:	

Part 6—Portability of Deceased Spousal Unused Exclusion (DSUE)

Portability Election

A decedent with a surviving spouse elects portability of the DSUE amount, if any, by completing and timely filing this return. No further action is required to elect portability of the DSUE amount to allow the surviving spouse to use the decedent's DSUE amount.

Section A. Opting Out of Portability

The estate of a decedent with a surviving spouse may opt out of electing portability of the DSUE amount. Check here and do not complete Sections B and C of Part 6 only if the estate opts **NOT** to elect portability of the DSUE amount. ☐

Section B. Qualified Domestic Trust (QDOT)

	Yes	No

Are any assets of the estate being transferred to a QDOT? . . . .

If "Yes," the DSUE amount portable to a surviving spouse (calculated in Section C, below) is preliminary and shall be redetermined at the time of the final distribution or other taxable event imposing estate tax under section 2056A. See instructions for more details.

Section C. DSUE Amount Portable to the Surviving Spouse (To be completed by the estate of a decedent making a portability election.)

Complete the following calculation to determine the DSUE amount that can be transferred to the surviving spouse.

1	Enter the amount from line 9d, Part 2—Tax Computation	1	
2	Reserved	2	
3	Enter the value of the cumulative lifetime gifts on which tax was paid or payable. See instructions . . .	3	
4	Add lines 1 and 3	4	
5	Enter amount from line 10, Part 2—Tax Computation	5	
6	Divide amount on line 5 by 40% (0.40) (do not enter less than zero)	6	
7	Subtract line 6 from line 4	7	
8	Enter the amount from line 5, Part 2—Tax Computation	8	
9	Subtract line 8 from line 7 (do not enter less than zero)	9	
10	DSUE amount portable to surviving spouse (Enter lesser of line 9 or line 9a, Part 2—Tax Computation) . .	10	

Section D. DSUE Amount Received From Predeceased Spouse(s) (To be completed by the estate of a deceased surviving spouse with DSUE amount from predeceased spouse(s))

Provide the following information to determine the DSUE amount received from deceased spouses.

A Name of Deceased Spouse (dates of death after December 31, 2010, only)	B Date of Death (enter as mm/dd/yy)	C Portability Election Made?		D If "Yes," DSUE Amount Received From Spouse	E DSUE Amount Applied by Decedent to Lifetime Gifts	F Year of Form 709 Reporting Use of DSUE Amount Listed in col. E	G Remaining DSUE Amount, if any (subtract col. E from col. D)
		Yes	No				
Part 1 — DSUE RECEIVED FROM LAST DECEASED SPOUSE							
Part 2 — DSUE RECEIVED FROM OTHER PREDECEASED SPOUSE(S) AND USED BY DECEDENT							
Total (for all DSUE amounts from predeceased spouse(s) applied) . .							

Add the amount from Part 1, column D, and the total from Part 2, column E. Enter the result on line 9b, Part 2—Tax Computation . . . . ▶

Estate of:

Decedent's social security number

SCHEDULE A—Real Estate

- For jointly owned property that must be disclosed on Schedule E, see instructions.
- Real estate that is part of a sole proprietorship should be shown on Schedule F.
- Real estate that is included in the gross estate under sections 2035, 2036, 2037, or 2038 should be shown on Schedule G.
- Real estate that is included in the gross estate under section 2041 should be shown on Schedule H.
- If you elect section 2032A valuation, you must complete Schedule A and Schedule A-1.

Note: If the value of the gross estate, together with the amount of adjusted taxable gifts, is less than the basic exclusion amount and Form 706 is being filed solely to elect portability of the DSUE amount, consideration should be given as to whether you are required to report the value of assets eligible for the marital or charitable deduction on this schedule. See the instructions for more information. If you are not required to report the value of an asset, identify the property but make no entries in the last three columns.

Item number	Description	Alternate valuation date	Alternate value	Value at date of death
1				
	Total from continuation schedules or additional statements attached to this schedule .			
TOTAL (Also enter on Part 5—Recapitulation, page 3, at item 1.)				

(If more space is needed, attach the continuation schedule from the end of this package or additional statements of the same size.)

Schedule A—Page 5

Decedent's social security number

Estate of:

SCHEDULE A-1—Section 2032A Valuation

Part 1. Type of Election (Before making an election, see the checklist in the instructions):

☐ **Protective election (Reg. section 20.2032A-8(b)).** Complete Part 2, line 1, and column A of lines 3 and 4. See instructions.

☐ **Regular election.** Complete all of Part 2 (including line 11, if applicable) and Part 3. See instructions.

Before completing Schedule A-1, see the instructions for the information and documents that must be included to make a valid election.

The election is not valid unless the agreement (that is, *Part 3. Agreement to Special Valuation Under Section 2032A)*:

• Is signed by each qualified heir with an interest in the specially valued property, and

• Is attached to this return when it is filed.

Part 2. Notice of Election (Reg. section 20.2032A-8(a)(3))

Note: All real property entered on lines 2 and 3 must also be entered on Schedules A, E, F, G, or H, as applicable.

1   Qualified use—check one ▶ ☐ Farm used for farming, or

☐ Trade or business other than farming

2   Real property used in a qualified use, passing to qualified heirs, and to be specially valued on this Form 706.

A Schedule and item number from Form 706	B Full value (without section 2032A(b)(3)(B) adjustment)	C Adjusted value (with section 2032A(b)(3)(B) adjustment)	D Value based on qualified use (without section 2032A(b)(3)(B) adjustment)
Totals			

Attach a legal description of all property listed on line 2.

Attach copies of appraisals showing the column B values for all property listed on line 2.

3   Real property used in a qualified use, passing to qualified heirs, but not specially valued on this Form 706.

A Schedule and item number from Form 706	B Full value (without section 2032A(b)(3)(B) adjustment)	C Adjusted value (with section 2032A(b)(3)(B) adjustment)	D Value based on qualified use (without section 2032A(b)(3)(B) adjustment)
Totals			

If you checked "Regular election," you must attach copies of appraisals showing the column B values for all property listed on line 3.

(continued on next page)

Schedule A-1—Page 6

| **Estate of:** | | **Decedent's social security number** | |

4 Personal property used in a qualified use and passing to qualified heirs.

A Schedule and item number from Form 706	B Adjusted value (with section 2032A(b)(3)(B) adjustment)	A (continued) Schedule and item number from Form 706	B (continued) Adjusted value (with section 2032A(b)(3)(B) adjustment)
		"Subtotal" from col. B, below left	
Subtotal		**Total adjusted value** . . .	

5 Enter the value of the total gross estate as adjusted under section 2032A(b)(3)(A). a _____

6 **Attach a description of the method used to determine the special value based on qualified use.**

7 Did the decedent and/or a member of his or her family own all property listed on line 2 for at least 5 of the 8 years immediately preceding the date of the decedent's death? . . . . | Yes | No |

8 Were there any periods during the 8-year period preceding the date of the decedent's death during which the decedent or a member of his or her family:

a Did not own the property listed on line 2? . . . .

b Did not use the property listed on line 2 in a qualified use? . . . .

c Did not materially participate in the operation of the farm or other business within the meaning of section 2032A(e)(6)? If you answered "Yes" to any of the above, attach a statement listing the periods. If applicable, describe whether the exceptions of sections 2032A(b)(4) or (5) are met.

9 **Attach affidavits describing the activities constituting material participation and the identity and relationship to the decedent of the material participants.**

10 Persons holding interests. Enter the requested information for each party who received any interest in the specially valued property. **(Each of the qualified heirs receiving an interest in the property must sign the agreement, to be found on Part 3 of this Schedule A-1, and the agreement must be filed with this return.)**

	Name	Address
A		
B		
C		
D		
E		
F		
G		
H		

	Identifying number	Relationship to decedent	Fair market value	Special-use value
A				
B				
C				
D				
E				
F				
G				
H				

You must attach a computation of the GST tax savings attributable to direct skips for each person listed above who is a skip person. See instructions.

11 **Woodlands election.** Check here a ☐ if you wish to make a Woodlands election as described in section 2032A(e)(13). Enter the schedule and item numbers from Form 706 of the property for which you are making this election a ----------------------------

Attach a statement explaining why you are entitled to make this election. The IRS may issue regulations that require more information to substantiate this election. You will be notified by the IRS if you must supply further information.

Schedule A-1—Page 7

	Decedent's social security number
Estate of:	

Part 3. Agreement to Special Valuation Under Section 2032A

There cannot be a valid election unless:

• The agreement is executed by each one of the qualified heirs, and

• The agreement is included with the estate tax return when the estate tax return is filed.

We (list all qualified heirs)

_____

_____ ,

being all the qualified heirs and (list all other persons having an interest in the property required to sign this agreement)

_____

_____ ,

being all other parties having interests in the property, which is qualified real property and which is valued under section 2032A, do

hereby approve of the election made by _____ ,

Executor/Administrator of the estate of _____ ,

pursuant to section 2032A to value said property on the basis of the qualified use to which the property is devoted and do hereby enter into this agreement pursuant to section 2032A(d).

The undersigned agree and consent to the application of subsection (c) of section 2032A with respect to all the property described on Form 706, Schedule A-1, Part 2, line 2, attached to this agreement. More specifically, the undersigned heirs expressly agree and consent to personal liability under subsection (c) of 2032A for the additional estate and GST taxes imposed by that subsection with respect to their respective interests in the above-described property in the event of certain early dispositions of the property or early cessation of the qualified use of the property. It is understood that if a qualified heir disposes of any interest in qualified real property to any member of his or her family, such member may thereafter be treated as the qualified heir with respect to such interest upon filing a Form 706-A, United States Additional Estate Tax Return, and a new agreement.

The undersigned interested parties who are not qualified heirs consent to the collection of any additional estate and GST taxes imposed under section 2032A(c) from the specially valued property.

If there is a disposition of any interest which passes, or has passed to him or her, or if there is a cessation of the qualified use of any specially valued property which passes or passed to him or her, each of the undersigned heirs agrees to file a Form 706-A, and pay any additional estate and GST taxes due within 6 months of the disposition or cessation.

It is understood by all interested parties that this agreement is a condition precedent to the election of special-use valuation under section 2032A and must be executed by every interested party even though that person may not have received the estate (or GST) tax benefits or be in possession of such property.

Each of the undersigned understands that by making this election, a lien will be created and recorded pursuant to section 6324B on the property referred to in this agreement for the adjusted tax differences with respect to the estate as defined in section 2032A(c)(2)(C).

As the interested parties, the undersigned designate the following individual as their agent for all dealings with the Internal Revenue Service concerning the continued qualification of the specially valued property under section 2032A and on all issues regarding the special lien under section 6324B. The agent is authorized to act for the parties with respect to all dealings with the Internal Revenue Service on matters affecting the qualified real property described earlier. This includes the authorization:

• To receive confidential information on all matters relating to continued qualification under section 2032A of the specially valued real property and on all matters relating to the special lien arising under section 6324B;

• To furnish the Internal Revenue Service with any requested information concerning the property;

• To notify the Internal Revenue Service of any disposition or cessation of qualified use of any part of the property;

• To receive, but not to endorse and collect, checks in payment of any refund of Internal Revenue taxes, penalties, or interest;

• To execute waivers (including offers of waivers) of restrictions on assessment or collection of deficiencies in tax and waivers of notice of disallowance of a claim for credit or refund; and

• To execute closing agreements under section 7121.

(continued on next page)

Schedule A-1—Page 8

160

Estate of:	Decedent's social security number

Part 3. Agreement to Special Valuation Under Section 2032A *(continued)*

• Other acts (specify) a _____

By signing this agreement, the agent agrees to provide the Internal Revenue Service with any requested information concerning this property and to notify the Internal Revenue Service of any disposition or cessation of the qualified use of any part of this property.

Name of Agent	Signature	Address

The property to which this agreement relates is listed in Form 706, United States Estate (and Generation-Skipping Transfer) Tax Return, and in the Notice of Election, along with its fair market value according to section 2031 and its special-use value according to section 2032A. The name, address, social security number, and interest (including the value) of each of the undersigned in this property are as set forth in the attached Notice of Election.

IN WITNESS WHEREOF, the undersigned have hereunto set their hands at _____ ,

this _____ day of _____ .

SIGNATURES OF EACH OF THE QUALIFIED HEIRS:

Signature of qualified heir	Signature of qualified heir
Signature of qualified heir	Signature of qualified heir
Signature of qualified heir	Signature of qualified heir
Signature of qualified heir	Signature of qualified heir
Signature of qualified heir	Signature of qualified heir
Signature of qualified heir	Signature of qualified heir

Signatures of other interested parties

Signatures of other interested parties

Schedule A-1—Page 9

Estate of:	Decedent's social security number

SCHEDULE B—Stocks and Bonds

(For jointly owned property that must be disclosed on Schedule E, see instructions.)

Note: If the value of the gross estate, together with the amount of adjusted taxable gifts, is less than the basic exclusion amount and Form 706 is being filed solely to elect portability of the DSUE amount, consideration should be given as to whether you are required to report the value of assets eligible for the marital or charitable deduction on this schedule. See the instructions for more information. If you are not required to report the value of an asset, identify the property but make no entries in the last four columns.

Item number	Description, including face amount of bonds or number of shares and par value for identification. Give CUSIP number. If trust, partnership, or closely held entity, give EIN.	Unit value	Alternate valuation date	Alternate value	Value at date of death
1	CUSIP number or EIN, where applicable				
	Total from continuation schedules (or additional statements) attached to this schedule .				
	TOTAL (Also enter on Part 5—Recapitulation, page 3, at item 2.)				

(If more space is needed, attach the continuation schedule from the end of this package or additional statements of the same size.)

Schedule B—Page 10

Estate of:	Decedent's social security number

SCHEDULE C—Mortgages, Notes, and Cash

(For jointly owned property that must be disclosed on Schedule E, see instructions.)

Note: If the value of the gross estate, together with the amount of adjusted taxable gifts, is less than the basic exclusion amount and Form 706 is being filed solely to elect portability of the DSUE amount, consideration should be given as to whether you are required to report the value of assets eligible for the marital or charitable deduction on this schedule. See the instructions for more information. If you are not required to report the value of an asset, identify the property but make no entries in the last three columns.

Item number	Description	Alternate valuation date	Alternate value	Value at date of death
1				
	Total from continuation schedules (or additional statements) attached to this schedule .			
	TOTAL (Also enter on Part 5—Recapitulation, page 3, at item 3.)			

(If more space is needed, attach the continuation schedule from the end of this package or additional statements of the same size.)

Schedule C—Page 11

	Decedent's social security number
Estate of:	

SCHEDULE D—Insurance on the Decedent's Life

You must list all policies on the life of the decedent and attach a Form 712 for each policy.

Note: If the value of the gross estate, together with the amount of adjusted taxable gifts, is less than the basic exclusion amount and Form 706 is being filed solely to elect portability of the DSUE amount, consideration should be given as to whether you are required to report the value of assets eligible for the marital or charitable deduction on this schedule. See the instructions for more information. If you are not required to report the value of an asset, identify the property but make no entries in the last three columns.

Item number	Description	Alternate valuation date	Alternate value	Value at date of death
1				
	Total from continuation schedules (or additional statements) attached to this schedule .			
	TOTAL (Also enter on Part 5—Recapitulation, page 3, at item 4.)			

(If more space is needed, attach the continuation schedule from the end of this package or additional statements of the same size.)

Schedule D—Page 12

Estate of:	**Decedent's social security number**

SCHEDULE E—Jointly Owned Property
(If you elect section 2032A valuation, you must complete Schedule E and Schedule A-1.)

PART 1. Qualified Joint Interests—Interests Held by the Decedent and His or Her Spouse as the Only Joint Tenants (Section 2040(b)(2))

Note: If the value of the gross estate, together with the amount of adjusted taxable gifts, is less than the basic exclusion amount and Form 706 is being filed solely to elect portability of the DSUE amount, consideration should be given as to whether you are required to report the value of assets eligible for the marital or charitable deduction on this schedule. See the instructions for more information. If you are not required to report the value of an asset, identify the property but make no entries in the last three columns.

Item number	Description. For securities, give CUSIP number. If trust, partnership, or closely held entity, give EIN.		Alternate valuation date	Alternate value	Value at date of death
1		CUSIP number or EIN, where applicable			
	Total from continuation schedules (or additional statements) attached to this schedule				
1a	Totals **1a**				
b	Amounts included in gross estate (one-half of line **1a**) **1b**				

PART 2. All Other Joint Interests

2a State the name and address of each surviving co-tenant. If there are more than three surviving co-tenants, list the additional co-tenants on an attached statement.

Name	Address (number and street, city, state, and ZIP code)
A.	
B.	
C.	

Item number	Enter letter for co-tenant	Description (including alternate valuation date, if any). For securities, give CUSIP number. If trust, partnership, or closely held entity, give EIN		Percentage includible	Includible alternate value	Includible value at date of death
1			CUSIP number or EIN, where applicable			
		Total from continuation schedules (or additional statements) attached to this schedule				
b		Total other joint interests **2b**				
3		**Total includible joint interests** (add lines 1b and 2b). Also enter on Part 5—Recapitulation, page 3, at item 5 . . . . **3**				

(If more space is needed, attach the continuation schedule from the end of this package or additional statements of the same size.)

Schedule E—Page 13

	Decedent's social security number
Estate of:	

SCHEDULE F—Other Miscellaneous Property Not Reportable Under Any Other Schedule
(For jointly owned property that must be disclosed on Schedule E, see instructions.)
(If you elect section 2032A valuation, you must complete Schedule F and Schedule A-1.)

Note: If the value of the gross estate, together with the amount of adjusted taxable gifts, is less than the basic exclusion amount and Form 706 is being filed solely to elect portability of the DSUE amount, consideration should be given as to whether you are required to report the value of assets eligible for the marital or charitable deduction on this schedule. See the instructions for more information. If you are not required to report the value of an asset, identify the property but make no entries in the last three columns.

		Yes	No
1	Did the decedent own any works of art, items, or any collections whose artistic or collectible value at date of death exceeded $3,000? . . . . If "Yes," submit full details on this schedule and attach appraisals.		
2	Has the decedent's estate, spouse, or any other person received (or will receive) any bonus or award as a result of the decedent's employment or death? . . . . If "Yes," submit full details on this schedule.		
3	Did the decedent at the time of death have, or have access to, a safe deposit box? . . . . If "Yes," state location, and if held jointly by decedent and another, state name and relationship of joint depositor.		

If any of the contents of the safe deposit box are omitted from the schedules in this return, explain fully why omitted.

Item number	Description. For securities, give CUSIP number. If trust, partnership, or closely held entity, give EIN	CUSIP number or EIN, where applicable	Alternate valuation date	Alternate value	Value at date of death
1					
	Total from continuation schedules (or additional statements) attached to this schedule .				
	TOTAL (Also enter on Part 5—Recapitulation, page 3, at item 6.)				

(If more space is needed, attach the continuation schedule from the end of this package or additional statements of the same size.)

Schedule F—Page 14

Estate of:

Decedent's social security number

SCHEDULE G—Transfers During Decedent's Life

(If you elect section 2032A valuation, you must complete Schedule G and Schedule A-1.)

Note: If the value of the gross estate, together with the amount of adjusted taxable gifts, is less than the basic exclusion amount and Form 706 is being filed solely to elect portability of the DSUE amount, consideration should be given as to whether you are required to report the value of assets eligible for the marital or charitable deduction on this schedule. See the instructions for more information. If you are not required to report the value of an asset, identify the property but make no entries in the last three columns.

Item number	Description. For securities, give CUSIP number. If trust, partnership, or closely held entity, give EIN	Alternate valuation date	Alternate value	Value at date of death
A.	Gift tax paid or payable by the decedent or the estate for all gifts made by the decedent or his or her spouse within 3 years before the decedent's death (section 2035(b))	X X X X X		
B.	Transfers includible under sections 2035(a), 2036, 2037, or 2038:			
1				
	Total from continuation schedules (or additional statements) attached to this schedule .			
TOTAL (Also enter on Part 5—Recapitulation, page 3, at item 7.)			

SCHEDULE H—Powers of Appointment

(Include "5 and 5 lapsing" powers (section 2041(b)(2)) held by the decedent.)
(If you elect section 2032A valuation, you must complete Schedule H and Schedule A-1.)

Note: If the value of the gross estate, together with the amount of adjusted taxable gifts, is less than the basic exclusion amount and Form 706 is being filed solely to elect portability of the DSUE amount, consideration should be given as to whether you are required to report the value of assets eligible for the marital or charitable deduction on this schedule. See the instructions for more information. If you are not required to report the value of an asset, identify the property but make no entries in the last three columns.

Item number	Description	Alternate valuation date	Alternate value	Value at date of death
1				
	Total from continuation schedules (or additional statements) attached to this schedule .			
TOTAL (Also enter on Part 5—Recapitulation, page 3, at item 8.)			

(If more space is needed, attach the continuation schedule from the end of this package or additional statements of the same size.)

Schedules G and H—Page 15

	Decedent's social security number
Estate of:	

SCHEDULE I—Annuities

Note: Generally, no exclusion is allowed for the estates of decedents dying after December 31, 1984. See instructions.

Note: If the value of the gross estate, together with the amount of adjusted taxable gifts, is less than the basic exclusion amount and Form 706 is being filed solely to elect portability of the DSUE amount, consideration should be given as to whether you are required to report the value of assets eligible for the marital or charitable deduction on this schedule. See the instructions for more information. If you are not required to report the value of an asset, identify the property but make no entries in the last three columns.

A   Are you excluding from the decedent's gross estate the value of a lump-sum distribution described in section 2039(f)(2) (as in effect before its repeal by the Deficit Reduction Act of 1984)? . . . .   **Yes**   **No**

      If "Yes," you must attach the information required by the instructions.

Item number	Description. Show the entire value of the annuity before any exclusions	Alternate valuation date	Includible alternate value	Includible value at date of death
1				
	Total from continuation schedules (or additional statements) attached to this schedule .			
	TOTAL (Also enter on Part 5—Recapitulation, page 3, at item 9.)			

(If more space is needed, attach the continuation schedule from the end of this package or additional statements of the same size.)

Schedule I—Page 16

168

Estate of:	Decedent's social security number

SCHEDULE J—Funeral Expenses and Expenses Incurred in Administering Property Subject to Claims

▲ **Use Schedule PC to make a protective claim for refund due to an expense not currently deductible.**
For such a claim, report the expense on Schedule J but without a value in the last column.

Note: Do not list expenses of administering property not subject to claims on this schedule. To report those expenses, see instructions.

If executors' commissions, attorney fees, etc., are claimed and allowed as a deduction for estate tax purposes, they are not allowable as a deduction in computing the taxable income of the estate for federal income tax purposes. They are allowable as an income tax deduction on Form 1041, U.S. Income Tax Return for Estates and Trusts, if a waiver is filed to forgo the deduction on Form 706. See the Instructions for Form 1041.

	Yes	No
Are you aware of any actual or potential reimbursement to the estate for any expense claimed as a deduction on this schedule?		

If "Yes," attach a statement describing the expense(s) subject to potential reimbursement. See instructions.

Item number	Description	Expense amount	Total amount
	A. Funeral expenses:		
1			
	Total funeral expenses . . . . ▲		

B. Administration expenses:

1 Executors' commissions—amount estimated/agreed upon/paid. (Strike out the words that do not apply.)		
2 Attorney fees—amount estimated/agreed upon/paid. (Strike out the words that do not apply.) . . .		
3 Accountant fees—amount estimated/agreed upon/paid. (Strike out the words that do not apply.) . .		

	4 Miscellaneous expenses:	Expense amount	
	Total miscellaneous expenses from continuation schedules (or additional statements) attached to this schedule		
	Total miscellaneous expenses . . . . ▲		
TOTAL (Also enter on Part 5—Recapitulation, page 3, at item 14.) . . . . ▲			

(If more space is needed, attach the continuation schedule from the end of this package or additional statements of the same size.)

Schedule J—Page 17

Estate of:	Decedent's social security number

SCHEDULE K—Debts of the Decedent, and Mortgages and Liens

a **Use Schedule PC to make a protective claim for refund due to a claim not currently deductible.**
For such a claim, report the expense on Schedule K but without a value in the last column.

	Yes	No
Are you aware of any actual or potential reimbursement to the estate for any debt of the decedent, mortgage, or lien claimed as a deduction on this schedule?		
If "Yes," attach a statement describing the items subject to potential reimbursement. See instructions.		
Are any of the items on this schedule deductible under Reg. section 20.2053-4(b) and Reg. section 20.2053-4(c)? . .		
If "Yes," attach a statement indicating the applicable provision and documenting the value of the claim.		

Item number	Debts of the Decedent—Creditor and nature of debt, and allowable death taxes	Amount
1		
	Total from continuation schedules (or additional statements) attached to this schedule	
	TOTAL (Also enter on Part 5—Recapitulation, page 3, at item 15.)	

Item number	Mortgages and Liens—Description	Amount
1		
	Total from continuation schedules (or additional statements) attached to this schedule	
	TOTAL (Also enter on Part 5—Recapitulation, page 3, at item 16.)	

(If more space is needed, attach the continuation schedule from the end of this package or additional statements of the same size.)

Schedule K—Page 18

Estate of:	Decedent's social security number

SCHEDULE L—Net Losses During Administration and Expenses Incurred in Administering Property Not Subject to Claims

ᵃ Use **Schedule PC** to make a protective claim for refund due to an expense not currently deductible.
For such expenses, report the expense on Schedule L but without a value in the last column.

Item number	Net losses during administration (**Note:** Do not deduct losses claimed on a federal income tax return.)	Amount
1		
	Total from continuation schedules (or additional statements) attached to this schedule	
TOTAL (Also enter on Part 5—Recapitulation, page 3, at item 19.)	

Item number	Expenses incurred in administering property not subject to claims. (Indicate whether estimated, agreed upon, or paid.)	Amount
1		
	Total from continuation schedules (or additional statements) attached to this schedule	
TOTAL (Also enter on Part 5—Recapitulation, page 3, at item 20.)	

(If more space is needed, attach the continuation schedule from the end of this package or additional statements of the same size.)

Schedule L—Page 19

171

Estate of:	Decedent's social security number

SCHEDULE M—Bequests, etc., to Surviving Spouse

Note: If the value of the gross estate, together with the amount of adjusted taxable gifts, is less than the basic exclusion amount and Form 706 is being filed solely to elect portability of the DSUE amount, consideration should be given as to whether you are required to report the value of assets eligible for the marital or charitable deduction on this schedule. See the instructions for more information. If you are not required to report the value of an asset, identify the property but make no entry in the last column.

		Yes	No
1	Did any property pass to the surviving spouse as a result of a qualified disclaimer? **1**		
	If "Yes," attach a copy of the written disclaimer required by section 2518(b).		
2a	In what country was the surviving spouse born? _____		
b	What is the surviving spouse's date of birth? _____		
c	Is the surviving spouse a U.S. citizen? **2c**		
d	If the surviving spouse is a naturalized citizen, when and where did the surviving spouse acquire citizenship?		
	_____		
e	If the surviving spouse is not a U.S. citizen, of what country is the surviving spouse a citizen? _____		
3	**Election Out of QTIP Treatment of Annuities.** Do you elect under section 2056(b)(7)(C)(ii) not to treat as qualified terminable interest property any joint and survivor annuities that are included in the gross estate and would otherwise be treated as qualified terminable interest property under section 2056(b)(7)(C)? See instructions **3**		

Item number	Description of property interests passing to surviving spouse. For securities, give CUSIP number. If trust, partnership, or closely held entity, give EIN	Amount
	QTIP property:	
A1		
	All other property:	
B1		
	Total from continuation schedules (or additional statements) attached to this schedule	
4	**Total** amount of property interests listed on Schedule M **4**	
5a	Federal estate taxes payable out of property interests listed on Schedule M .	**5a**	
b	Other death taxes payable out of property interests listed on Schedule M . .	**5b**	
c	Federal and state GST taxes payable out of property interests listed on Schedule M	**5c**	
d	Add items 5a, 5b, and 5c **5d**	
6	Net amount of property interests listed on Schedule M (subtract item 5d from item 4). Also enter on Part 5—Recapitulation, page 3, at item 21 . . . . **6**	

(If more space is needed, attach the continuation schedule from the end of this package or additional statements of the same size.)

Schedule M—Page 20

Form 709

United States Gift (and Generation-Skipping Transfer) Tax Return

OMB No. 1545-0020

▶ Go to *www.irs.gov/Form709* for instructions and the latest information.

(For gifts made during calendar year 2021)

▶ See instructions.

2021

Department of the Treasury
Internal Revenue Service

Part 1—General Information

1 Donor's first name and middle initial	**2** Donor's last name	**3** Donor's social security number
4 Address (number, street, and apartment number)		**5** Legal residence (domicile)
6 City or town, state or province, country, and ZIP or foreign postal code		**7** Citizenship (see instructions)

		Yes	No
8	If the donor died during the year, check here ▶ ☐ and enter date of death _____ , _____ .		
9	If you extended the time to file this Form 709, check here ▶ ☐		
10	Enter the total number of donees listed on Schedule A. Count each person only once ▶		
11a	Have you (the donor) previously filed a Form 709 (or 709-A) for any other year? If "No," skip line 11b		
b	Has your address changed since you last filed Form 709 (or 709-A)?		
12	**Gifts by husband or wife to third parties.** Do you consent to have the gifts (including generation-skipping transfers) made by you and by your spouse to third parties during the calendar year considered as made one-half by each of you? (See instructions.) (If the answer is "Yes," the following information must be furnished and your spouse must sign the consent shown below. **If the answer is "No," skip lines 13–18.)**		

13 Name of consenting spouse	**14** SSN		

		Yes	No
15	Were you married to one another during the entire calendar year? See instructions		
16	If line 15 is "No," check whether ☐ married ☐ divorced or ☐ widowed/deceased, and give date. See instructions ▶		
17	Will a gift tax return for this year be filed by your spouse? If "Yes," mail both returns in the same envelope		

18 **Consent of Spouse.** I consent to have the gifts (and generation-skipping transfers) made by me and by my spouse to third parties during the calendar year considered as made one-half by each of us. We are both aware of the joint and several liability for tax created by the execution of this consent.

Consenting spouse's signature ▶   Date ▶

19 Have you applied a DSUE amount received from a predeceased spouse to a gift or gifts reported on this or a previous Form 709? If "Yes," complete Schedule C . . . .

Part 2—Tax Computation

1	Enter the amount from Schedule A, Part 4, line 11	**1**	
2	Enter the amount from Schedule B, line 3	**2**	
3	Total taxable gifts. Add lines 1 and 2	**3**	
4	Tax computed on amount on line 3 (see *Table for Computing Gift Tax* in instructions)	**4**	
5	Tax computed on amount on line 2 (see *Table for Computing Gift Tax* in instructions)	**5**	
6	Balance. Subtract line 5 from line 4	**6**	
7	Applicable credit amount. If donor has DSUE amount from predeceased spouse(s) or Restored Exclusion Amount, enter amount from Schedule C, line 5; otherwise, see instructions	**7**	
8	Enter the applicable credit against tax allowable for all prior periods (from Sch. B, line 1, col. C) . . .	**8**	
9	Balance. Subtract line 8 from line 7. Do not enter less than zero	**9**	
10	Enter 20% (0.20) of the amount allowed as a specific exemption for gifts made after September 8, 1976, and before January 1, 1977. See instructions	**10**	
11	Balance. Subtract line 10 from line 9. Do not enter less than zero	**11**	
12	Applicable credit. Enter the smaller of line 6 or line 11	**12**	
13	Credit for foreign gift taxes (see instructions)	**13**	
14	Total credits. Add lines 12 and 13	**14**	
15	Balance. Subtract line 14 from line 6. Do not enter less than zero	**15**	
16	Generation-skipping transfer taxes (from Schedule D, Part 3, col. G, total)	**16**	
17	Total tax. Add lines 15 and 16	**17**	
18	Gift and generation-skipping transfer taxes prepaid with extension of time to file	**18**	
19	If line 18 is less than line 17, enter **balance due.** See instructions	**19**	
20	If line 18 is greater than line 17, enter **amount to be refunded**	**20**	

Sign Here

Under penalties of perjury, I declare that I have examined this return, including any accompanying schedules and statements, and to the best of my knowledge and belief, it is true, correct, and complete. Declaration of preparer (other than donor) is based on all information of which preparer has any knowledge.

May the IRS discuss this return with the preparer shown below? See instructions. ☐ **Yes** ☐ **No**

▶ Signature of donor   Date

Paid Preparer Use Only

Print/Type preparer's name	Preparer's signature	Date	Check ☐ if self-employed	PTIN
Firm's name ▶			Firm's EIN ▶	
Firm's address ▶			Phone no.	

Attach check or money order here.

For Disclosure, Privacy Act, and Paperwork Reduction Act Notice, see the instructions for this form.   Cat. No. 16783M   Form **709** (2021)

Estate of:	Decedent's social security number

SCHEDULE O—Charitable, Public, and Similar Gifts and Bequests

Note: If the value of the gross estate, together with the amount of adjusted taxable gifts, is less than the basic exclusion amount and Form 706 is being filed solely to elect portability of the DSUE amount, consideration should be given as to whether you are required to report the value of assets eligible for the marital or charitable deduction on this schedule. See the instructions for more information. If you are not required to report the value of an asset, identify the property but make no entry in the last column.

		Yes	No
1a	If the transfer was made by will, has any action been instituted to contest or have interpreted any of its provisions affecting the charitable deductions claimed in this schedule? . . . . If "Yes," full details must be submitted with this schedule.		
b	According to the information and belief of the person or persons filing this return, is any such action planned? . If "Yes," full details must be submitted with this schedule.		
2	Did any property pass to charity as the result of a qualified disclaimer? . . . . If "Yes," attach a copy of the written disclaimer required by section 2518(b).		

Item number	Name and address of beneficiary	Character of institution	Amount
1			
	Total from continuation schedules (or additional statements) attached to this schedule		

3	Total	**3**	
4a	Federal estate tax payable out of property interests listed above	**4a**	
b	Other death taxes payable out of property interests listed above	**4b**	
c	Federal and state GST taxes payable out of property interests listed above .	**4c**	
d	Add items 4a, 4b, and 4c	**4d**	
5	Net value of property interests listed above (subtract item 4d from item 3). Also enter on Part 5—Recapitulation, page 3, at item 22	**5**	

(If more space is needed, attach the continuation schedule from the end of this package or additional statements of the same size.)

Schedule O—Page 21

Estate of:	Decedent's social security number

SCHEDULE P—Credit for Foreign Death Taxes

List all foreign countries to which death taxes have been paid and for which a credit is claimed on this return.

If a credit is claimed for death taxes paid to more than one foreign country, compute the credit for taxes paid to one country on this sheet and attach a separate copy of Schedule P for each of the other countries.

The credit computed on this sheet is for the _____
(Name of death tax or taxes)

_____ imposed in _____
(Name of country)

Credit is computed under the _____
(Insert title of treaty or statute)

Citizenship (nationality) of decedent at time of death _____

(All amounts and values must be entered in U.S. money.)		
1 Total of estate, inheritance, legacy, and succession taxes imposed in the country named above attributable to property situated in that country, subjected to these taxes, and included in the gross estate (as defined by statute) .	1	
2 Value of the gross estate (adjusted, if necessary, according to the instructions)	2	
3 Value of property situated in that country, subjected to death taxes imposed in that country, and included in the gross estate (adjusted, if necessary, according to the instructions)	3	
4 Tax imposed by section 2001 reduced by the total credits claimed under sections 2010 and 2012 (see instructions)	4	
5 Amount of federal estate tax attributable to property specified at item 3. (Divide item 3 by item 2 and multiply the result by item 4.)	5	
6 Credit for death taxes imposed in the country named above (the smaller of item 1 or item 5). Also enter on line 13 of Part 2—Tax Computation	6	

SCHEDULE Q—Credit for Tax on Prior Transfers

Part 1. Transferor Information

	Name of transferor	Social security number	IRS office where estate tax return was filed	Date of death
A				
B				
C				

Check here a ☐ if section 2013(f) (special valuation of farm, etc., real property) adjustments to the computation of the credit were made. See instructions.

Part 2. Computation of Credit *(see instructions)*

Item	Transferor			Total A, B, and C
	A	B	C	
1 Transferee's tax as apportioned (from worksheet, (line 7 ÷ line 8) × line 35 for each column)				
2 Transferor's tax (from each column of worksheet, line 20)				
3 Maximum amount before percentage requirement (for each column, enter amount from line 1 or line 2, whichever is smaller)				
4 Percentage allowed (each column) (see instructions)	%	%	%	
5 Credit allowable (line 3 × line 4 for each column) .				
6 TOTAL credit allowable (add columns A, B, and C of line 5). Enter here and on line 14 of Part 2—Tax Computation				

Estate of:	Decedent's social security number

SCHEDULE R—Generation-Skipping Transfer Tax

Note: To avoid application of the deemed allocation rules, Form 706 and Schedule R should be filed to allocate the GST exemption to trusts that may later have taxable terminations or distributions under section 2612 even if the form is not required to be filed to report estate or GST tax.

The GST tax is imposed on taxable transfers of interests in property located outside the United States as well as property located inside the United States. See instructions.

Part 1. GST Exemption Reconciliation (Section 2631) and Special QTIP Election (Section 2652(a)(3))

You no longer need to check a box to make a section 2652(a)(3) (special QTIP) election. If you list qualifying property in Part 1, line 9, below, you will be considered to have made this election. See instructions for details.

1	Maximum allowable GST exemption	1
2	Total GST exemption allocated by the decedent against decedent's lifetime transfers	2
3	Total GST exemption allocated by the executor, using Form 709, against decedent's lifetime transfers	3
4	GST exemption allocated on line 6 of Schedule R, Part 2	4
5	GST exemption allocated on line 6 of Schedule R, Part 3	5
6	Total GST exemption allocated on line 4 of Schedule(s) R-1	6
7	Total GST exemption allocated to inter vivos transfers and direct skips (add lines 2–6)	7
8	GST exemption available to allocate to trusts and section 2032A interests (subtract line 7 from line 1)	8

9 Allocation of GST exemption to trusts (as defined for GST tax purposes):

A Name of trust	B Trust's EIN (if any)	C GST exemption allocated on lines 2–6 above (see instructions)	D Additional GST exemption allocated (see instructions)	E Trust's inclusion ratio (optional) (see instructions)

9D **Total.** May not exceed line 8 above	**9D**	
10 GST exemption available to allocate to section 2032A interests received by individual beneficiaries (subtract line 9D from line 8). You must attach special-use allocation statement. See instructions .	**10**	

Schedule R—Page 23

Estate of:

Decedent's social security number

Part 2. Direct Skips Where the Property Interests Transferred Bear the GST Tax on the Direct Skips

Name of skip person	Description of property interest transferred	Estate tax value

1	Total estate tax values of all property interests listed above	1	
2	Estate taxes, state death taxes, and other charges borne by the property interests listed above . .	2	
3	GST taxes borne by the property interests listed above but imposed on direct skips other than those shown on this Part 2 (see instructions)	3	
4	Total fixed taxes and other charges (add lines 2 and 3)	4	
5	Total tentative maximum direct skips (subtract line 4 from line 1)	5	
6	GST exemption allocated	6	
7	Subtract line 6 from line 5	7	
8	GST tax due (divide line 7 by 3.5)	8	
9	Enter the amount from line 8 of Schedule R, Part 3	9	
10	**Total GST taxes payable by the estate** (add lines 8 and 9). Enter here and on line 17 of Part 2—Tax Computation	10	

Schedule R—Page 24

	Decedent's social security number
Estate of:	

Part 3. Direct Skips Where the Property Interests Transferred Do Not Bear the GST Tax on the Direct Skips

Name of skip person	Description of property interest transferred	Estate tax value

1 Total estate tax values of all property interests listed above	**1**	
2 Estate taxes, state death taxes, and other charges borne by the property interests listed above . .	**2**	
3 GST taxes borne by the property interests listed above but imposed on direct skips other than those shown on this Part 3 (see instructions)	**3**	
4 Total fixed taxes and other charges (add lines 2 and 3)	**4**	
5 Total tentative maximum direct skips (subtract line 4 from line 1)	**5**	
6 GST exemption allocated	**6**	
7 Subtract line 6 from line 5	**7**	
8 GST tax due (multiply line 7 by 0.40). Enter here and on Schedule R, Part 2, line 9	**8**	

Schedule R—Page 25

Estate of:	Decedent's social security number

SCHEDULE U—Qualified Conservation Easement Exclusion

Part 1. Election

Note: The executor is deemed to have made the election under section 2031(c)(6) if he or she files Schedule U and excludes any qualifying conservation easements from the gross estate.

Part 2. General Qualifications

1 Describe the land subject to the qualified conservation easement. See instructions _____

2 Did the decedent or a member of the decedent's family own the land described above during the 3-year period ending on the date of the decedent's death? . . . . ☐ Yes ☐ No

3 Describe the conservation easement with regard to which the exclusion is being claimed. See instructions.

Part 3. Computation of Exclusion

4	Estate tax value of the land subject to the qualified conservation easement (see instructions) .			**4**	
5	Date of death value of any easements granted prior to decedent's death and included on line 10 below (see instructions)	**5**			
6	Add lines 4 and 5	**6**			
7	Value of retained development rights on the land (see instructions)	**7**			
8	Subtract line 7 from line 6	**8**			
9	Multiply line 8 by 30% (0.30)	**9**			
10	Value of qualified conservation easement for which the exclusion is being claimed (see instructions)	**10**			
	Note: If line 10 is less than line 9, continue with line 11. If line 10 is equal to or more than line 9, skip lines 11 through 13, enter "0.40" on line 14, and complete the schedule.				
11	Divide line 10 by line 8. Figure to 3 decimal places (for example, "0.123")	**11**			
	Note: If line 11 is equal to or less than 0.100, stop here; the estate does not qualify for the conservation easement exclusion.				
12	Subtract line 11 from 0.300. Enter the answer in hundredths by rounding any thousandths up to the next higher hundredth (that is, 0.030 = 0.03, but 0.031 = 0.04)	**12**			
13	Multiply line 12 by 2.0	**13**			
14	Subtract line 13 from 0.40	**14**			
15	Deduction under section 2055(f) for the conservation easement (see instructions)	**15**			
16	Amount of indebtedness on the land (see instructions)	**16**			
17	Total reductions in value (add lines 7, 15, and 16)			**17**	
18	Net value of land (subtract line 17 from line 4)			**18**	
19	Multiply line 18 by line 14			**19**	
20	Enter the smaller of line 19 or the exclusion limitation. See instructions. Also enter this amount on item 12, Part 5—Recapitulation, page 3			**20**	

Schedule U—Page 26

Protective Claim for Refund

ᵃ **To be used for decedents dying after December 31, 2011. File 2 copies of this schedule with Form 706 for each pending claim or expense under section 2053.**

OMB No. 1545-0015

- Timely filing a protective claim for refund preserves the estate's right to claim a refund based on the amount of an unresolved claim or expense that may not become deductible under section 2053 until after the limitation period ends.
- Schedule PC can be used to file a protective claim for refund and, once the claim or expense becomes deductible, Schedule PC can be used to notify the IRS that a refund is being claimed.
- Schedule PC can be used by the estate of a decedent dying after 2011.
- Schedule PC must be filed with Form 706 and cannot be filed separately. (To file a protective claim for refund or notify the IRS that a refund is being claimed in a form separate from the Form 706, instead use Form 843, Claim for Refund and Request for Abatement.)
- Each separate claim or expense requires a separate Schedule PC (or Form 843, if not filed with Form 706).
- Schedule PC must be filed in duplicate (two copies) for each separate claim or expense.

Part 1. General Information

1. Name of decedent	2. Decedent's social security no.
3. Name of fiduciary	4. Date of death
5a. Address (number, street, and room or suite no.)	5b. Room or suite no.
5c. City or town, state, and ZIP or postal code	6. Daytime telephone number

7. Number of Claims. Enter number of Schedules PC being filed with Form 706. _____

If the number is greater than one OR if another Schedule PC or Form 843 was previously filed by or on behalf of the estate, complete Part 3 of this Schedule PC.

8. Fiduciary ☐ Check here if this Schedule PC is being filed with the original Form 706 or is being filed by the same fiduciary who filed the original Form 706 for decedent's estate. If a different fiduciary is filing this Schedule PC, see instructions for establishing the legal authority to pursue the claim for refund on behalf of the estate.

Part 2. Claim Information

Check the box that applies to this claim for refund.

a. ☐ Protective claim for refund made for unresolved claim or expense.

   Amount in contest: _____

b. ☐ Partial refund claimed: partial resolution and/or satisfaction of claim or expense for which a protective claim for refund has been filed previously.

   Date protective claim for refund filed for this claim or expense: _____

   Amount of claim or expense partially resolved and/or satisfied and presently claimed as a deduction under section 2053 (do not include amounts previously deducted): _____

c. ☐ Full and final refund claimed for this claim or expense: resolution and/or satisfaction of claim or expense for which a protective claim for refund has been filed previously.

   Date protective claim for refund filed for this claim or expense: _____

   Amount of claim or expense finally resolved and/or satisfied and presently claimed as a deduction under section 2053 (do not include amounts previously deducted): _____

Schedule PC—Page 27

Estate of:

Decedent's social security number

A Form 706 Schedule and Item number	**B** **Identification of the claim** • Name or names of the claimant(s) • Basis of the claim or other description of the pending claim or expense • Reasons and contingencies delaying resolution • Status of contested matters • Attach copies of relevant pleadings or other documents	**C** Amount, if any, deducted under Treas. Reg. sections 20.2053-1(d)(4) or 20.2053-4(b) or (c) for the identified claim or expense	**D** Amount presently claimed as a deduction under section 2053 for the identified claim	**E** Ancillary expenses estimated/agreed upon/paid (Please indicate)	**F** Amount of tax to be refunded

Part 3. Other Schedules PC and Forms 843 Filed by Estate

If a Schedule PC or Form 843 was previously filed by the estate, complete Part 3 to identify each claim for refund reported.

A Date of death	**B** Internal Revenue office where filed	**C** Date filed	**D** Indicate whether (1) Protective Claim for Refund, (2) Partial Claim for Refund, or (3) Full and Final Claim for Refund	**E** Amount in Contest
1				

To inquire about the receipt and/or processing of the protective claim for refund, please call 866-699-4083.

(Make copies of this schedule before completing it if you will need more than one schedule.)

	Decedent's social security number
Estate of:	

CONTINUATION SCHEDULE

Continuation of Schedule _____
(Enter letter of schedule you are continuing.)

Item number	Description. For securities, give CUSIP number. If trust, partnership, or closely held entity, give EIN.	Unit value (Sch. B, E, or G only)	Alternate valuation date	Alternate value	Value at date of death or amount deductible
TOTAL (Carry forward to main schedule.)					

Continuation Schedule—Page 29

182

My purpose of DEAR EXECUTOR: A WORKBOOK is to help you (writer) collect the information that your executor will need when completing your IRS Form 706. It is not to serve as your tax accountant who will complete the tax form or your attorney who will do your legal work.

Go to your accountant or lawyer or have your executor go to them for those needs. I am not able knowledge-wise or with proper credentials.

With my best regards,

Mary Jeanne Anderson Jones

_____

Signed

_____

Dated

AUTHOR'S BIO

I, Mary Jeanne Anderson Jones, the author of *DEAR EXECUTOR: A WORKBOOK*, at 87 years of age, am of the generation most needy of this type of discipline, the preparation of materials necessary to eventually settle his or her estate. The intent with *DEAR EXECUTOR: A WORKBOOK* is not to be morbid, but to be practical and helpful.

When this all started, it was past time for me to update my own will and 4-codicil trust, both executed originally in 1996 or slightly later, as well as my healthcare directives, and to change my executor from a son who lives in Florida to a daughter who lives 10 minutes away from me. You would think that a retired investment adviser who preached to her clients the necessity of providing all-important information about her wishes about her obit, memorial service, burial or cremation, and then about assets and liabilities that would be essential after death for the Probate Court, or whatever court the person's state provided to settle her estate, would be up-to-date on the essentials that her executor would need in settling her estate. But I was not then, nor am I now.

Practice what I say, not what I do.

My lack of discipline in this area is the Number One Reason that I decided *DEAR EXECUTOR* had to be written. It is the descendant of the LOCATIONS LIST that I used while serving as an investment adviser, but is far more detailed and demanding. My hope is that it will serve as a great incentive for anyone who purchases it and goes to the trouble of filling out the pertinent information. I wanted it to be a workbook, soft cover, non-threatening, and easy to work with by people of all ages, not just by my generation.

It has been many years since I last published a book. While living near Charlottesville, Virginia, I had co-authored a book with the chairman of the University's Pharmacology Department. The Department of Pharmacology at the University, published it as a biographical study of the eleven chairmen of the department, dating back to Thomas Jefferson's era and then continuing on to the mid 1960s. My first solo work was *Congregational Commonwealth, Connecticut, 1636-1662*, which tells the story of the founding of Connecticut long ago. Wesleyan University Press published it at the time when I had received my MA from the University of Virginia and had moved to a lovely village near Heidelberg, Germany, with my husband and three young children, courtesy of Uncle Sam.

Upon our return to the States I settled our family, got bored, and joined the investment world as a securities analyst. While there I did nothing in the field of publications, except for writing buy and sell investment recommendations to clients and later personal financial letters, again to clients. I also studied and became an Enrolled Agent of the IRS for ten years, legally able to represent clients in court just as lawyers and CPAs do, and a Chartered Financial Analyst.

Then many years later came the idea about *DEAR EXECUTOR: A WORKBOOK* and the probability of its becoming an ebook as well as a paperback. It borrows from the experience I had as an Enrolled Agent and the tax knowledge it entailed. It also draws from the investment world in asking for assets and liabilities and in understanding peoples' financial situations.

Hopefully, *DEAR EXECUTOR:* will serve as an incentive for the financial member of a family to share his/her knowledge with the other half and so not to leave the family unknowing about their situation after his/her death and in a chaotic frame of mind, facing the unknown.